*A
Victorian
Album*

A Victorian Album

62372

Some Lady Novelists of the Period

& Lucy Poate Stebbins

Columbia University Press, New York

1946

*"This book is dedicated to my dear husband
by her who best knows his value."*

Preface

THE LONG TRAIN of inquiries which resulted in this little book began in an idle, summer's day discussion concerning the blighting effect of the Victorian moral code on the work of women novelists. This question, when subsequently applied to the lives and writings of a large number of these ladies, brought a wide variety of answers, although at the outset we must in honor confess that most of these authors were revealed as social tyrants rather than as victims of tyranny. Although the charge against the Victorian code could not be clearly proved, much that was unexpected and entertaining emerged, while the purpose of study broadened into an effort to understand the relation between the individual lives and works of representative women writers of fiction.

In the case of obscure novelists, source material is to be found only in great libraries to which comparatively few readers have access. Even when ample opportunity is given to the research worker, it is no easy task to sift the truth from varying and frequently untrustworthy reports furnished by partial friends and relatives to the publishers of biographical data. To read the work of these women was a labor of many years, so numerous were the scribblers, so prodigious their exertions. But their life stories, enriched by the naïve self-revelations characteristic of the Victorians, and correlated with their novels, furnished an absorbing psychological adventure. How work grows out of life can never fail to possess an enthralling human interest, and the connection may be traced with some assurance when a novelist and her novels are the subjects pursued by one who in her day has written many novels.

It has been convenient to group our authors roughly into classes and to select representatives from each of them; this method has resulted in the omission of several familiar names. Other authors were exempted because their writing of novels was incidental, merely an interruption of a characteristic career: such were the unhappy Letitia Landon, who was a popular poetess; the magnificent Lady Blessington, who was more remarkable as an editor and a hostess than as a fiction writer; and Charlotte M. Yonge, whose favorite field was the juvenile.

But though no further warrant is needed for a chapter on obscure novelists of the nineteenth century, an apology may be necessary for the following studies of the four great writers, Charlotte Brontë, Elizabeth Gaskell, George Eliot, and Margaret Oliphant.

The pilgrimage of Charlotte Brontë through the visible world has been told often and well; no study of the _juvenilia_ can alter the story of her life as it passed under human eyes. Yet no biographer, however gifted, honest, and sympathetic, has been able to do justice to Charlotte Brontë, because it is impossible to understand her mature works without a thorough study of her youthful writings. With an enthusiasm no doubt pardonable in the explorer but much to be regretted in the scholar recent students of the _juvenilia_ have attributed all the elements in Charlotte's finished novels to her crude early attempts. It has been our more reasonable purpose to show the process by which various fantasies of her childhood and protracted adolescence were purged and refashioned until they could be incorporated in her adult work.

Elizabeth Gaskell's biography has never been written. She was perhaps the most limpid character in letters: her life explains her works; her books reveal the woman.

The attempt to trace the relation between George Eliot's subjective life and her writings has resulted in what may be considered by her partisans as graceless iconoclasm. The author had no wish to demolish an idol, and acknowledges a personal regret. But George Eliot, as a lover of justice and a defender of the intellectual process, could not have censured the honesty of the search.

No biography of Margaret Oliphant has as yet been written. Of her life, little was ever widely known and that little has been forgotten with the enormous bulk of her writings. She was a woman of great ability and of large accomplishments, the most inventive and the most versatile novelist of the century, a Victorian of the Victorians. Her private life was characterized by an almost suicidal suppression of all natural instincts except the maternal. She was less strict with her public than with herself; her novels are tolerant; her subtle humor is only mildly caustic. It may be that Margaret Oliphant is our best example of the woman novelist as victim, but readers of the present sketch must determine for themselves whether she was the victim of her mother or of her sons; John Calvin's or Victoria's.

One word more in explanation: I owe no allegiance to any of the several contemporary schools of psychology. The phenomena with which I have been dealing were familiar to literary artists long before the medical profession began to concern itself with them. This is not said in depreciation of the specialized labors of modern psy-

chologists, but is intended merely to emphasize the independence of
my own interpretations.

The dedication has been borrowed from Mrs. Gaskell's novel,
Sylvia's Lovers.

LUCY POATE STEBBINS

Cambridge
1946

Contents

Contents

Those who would seek to know the cause
of the feelings *and* actions *of men and women*
must go back to childhood and its impressions
ANNA MARIA HALL

A Ladies' Miscellany

PERHAPS NO NOVELIST can answer satisfactorily the seemingly innocuous question: Why do women write? The surface reasons which are valid today—the need for money, the hunger for self-expression, ambition—were more powerful in the Victorian lady, to whom at best few occupations lay open. If she needed money for herself or her children, she was more likely to get it by writing a novel than by attempting anything else within her social range. In the early part of the century it was considered ill-bred to write under one's own name, at any rate until after success had visited early efforts; but the secret was not closely guarded, and the ambition to be known and praised was, so George Eliot flatly declared, three times as powerful as the desire for money. But we must not forget that, besides those novelists who struggled for reputation or for cash, there were always a few noble-hearted, if wrong-headed, women who wrote principally to support a Cause.

Many a Victorian lady felt all these urges but never penned a line except in her letters and account books. In youth she had expressed her artistic yearnings by playing the piano or sketching a haymow in the morning and the same haymow in late afternoon; when she was old, she worked contentedly in Berlin wools. If she was ambitious, she might prod an indolent relative into Parliament; her philanthropic impulses could be choked by distributing the inevitable flannel petticoats at Christmas. The woman who became a novelist found one or more such urges not only strong but compulsive; she *must* make money, *must* express herself, *must* redress a social wrong. George Eliot refused to believe that a happy wife and mother would turn novelist unless driven by "some hereditary organic tendency, stronger even than the domestic," an opinion we will not attempt to clarify. She added more intelligibly that women wrote because they were unhappy.

Most of the women whom we shall consider in this chapter were married and many of them were mothers of large families. Thus the important business of their lives was to protect the British Home; novel-writing was a subsidiary occupation undertaken in the hope of propping up household finances. It was the honest, if unaimiable, conviction of these homemaking novelists that the more rigid the rules of convention, the stronger their position as well-behaved matrons. Most of them were daughters, sisters, wives, or mothers of ministers; in clerical society a novelist might occupy all four of these lofty stations. The pulpit nearly belonged to such women, and it was natural that they should preach in their writings what they heard on Sunday from their menfolk. In the three-volume novel of the first half of the century, the substance of one volume was usually devoted to moral utterances. These novelists had neither leisure nor inclination to think on abstract problems; they followed the profession in their opposition to biblical research and the discoveries of science.

Frequently these ladies uttered a reasonable plaint over the wretched education which had been doled out to them in contrast to expensive instruction which had been wasted on their brothers. But the insufficient schooling of other little girls to whom they were not related did not trouble them. Those matrons whose books sold well worked hard for the bill which would give married women the right to control their own property, but in most matters they found their liberty sufficient; they were not altruists, and, possessing freedom, united in their opposition to the coarse impropriety of Women's Rights. Their views were rigidly personal; they wanted their sons and daughters, and even their nephews and nieces, to be prosperous and happy, but it was apparent to them that God had ordained the classes of English society in a highly commendable fashion: His manifest intentions ought to be accepted as divine justice. What He considered best for a clergyman's wife would be thoroughly bad for a bricklayer's daughter.

These excellent ladies believed that God watched, punished, and rewarded; they were always conscious of His supervision and knew that He approved their firm dealings with the vices and virtues of their characters. Their long novels seldom closed with marriage; frequently it was the writer's task to lay the genteel heroine in the family vault; to deposit her in the churchyard, if she were Lower or Lower Middle; in an extreme case to bury her with her fatherless child in the solitary valley remote from human eyes.

In many cases, the lady novelist had reached middle age when she began to write; before her mature eyes life unrolled itself in leisurely sequences; but the last landmark on the horizon's verge was not the grave; it was a gate leading to the country beyond; that might be Heaven, it might be Hell—the lady novelist knew the exact bourne from which her several characters would not return.

When we review the lives of these writers after the lapse of generations, we encounter many variants, some peculiar to the time and class in which the future authoress happened to be born, but many of them possible in any period. The culture of the family, the number of children and the position the little girl occupied among them, the old nurse, the love the father and mother had for each other and for their children, the church, the school—such elements determined the course of the girl who was destined to turn novelist. The spirit, reaching out tentacles, appropriated what it chose from the environment and gradually shaped the form on which it had, in the unconscious depths, determined.

Fifty years have passed since the death of Margaret Oliphant, the last but one of the novelists with whom this book is concerned; the revolt against Victorianism has long subsided and we should be able to see these women without prejudice. The only way to understand them is to relive their lives—difficult, sorrow laden, but never lacking energy—to read their novels, and, learning something of their world, measure its virtues and follies by our own.

With apologies for the arbitrary nature of the classification—admittedly only one of the many possible—I have grouped together first, those gifted women who could live in accordance with Victorian standards only by the sternest self-repression; second, the pseudo-romancists, creators of an unreal world in which they and their sentimental readers took a sensuous pleasure; third, those unpretentious, indefatigable business women who worked, sometimes alone, sometimes in partnership with a son or husband—never, I believe, with another woman; last, a few words on the aristocrat in letters.

BECAUSE THE ORIGINAL PURPOSE of this study was to discover trammeled souls, we will consider first the little group of rebels and in the forefront Eliza Lynn Linton, born Eliza Lynn, once a brave young creature, whom the experiences of a lifetime tamed into submissive, dreary age.

The Lynns were Church people, well-to-do and indisputably Upper Middle Class. Eliza's grandfather was the Bishop of Carlisle; her father held three livings at one time and owned Gads Hill, the fine house which Dickens coveted in his youthful poverty and bought in his prosperity.

The atmosphere of the Lynn household had not the pious tranquillity suggested by its clerical connections. Eliza was the youngest of twelve sturdy, handsome children. Before she was out of her cradle, her mother died, leaving her baby to fight her way up among turbulent brothers and sisters. She was a bold, provoking little creature and her elders were rough and pitiless. The father, no mean scholar, was too indolent to teach his daughters and too parsimonious to send them to school; Eliza began very early to resent his omissions and certain eccentricities such as prayers at inconvenient seasons. The love which her emotional young heart would have lavished on a good father was stored up and years later poured out upon the aging Landor. In her warring childhood she spent her affections on the one brother and sister who were kind to her, and on the image of the mother she had never known.

The older girls of the family were expected to instruct the younger, but Eliza learned nothing beyond sewing, which she, like almost every woman writer of the century, loathed in youth and valued as a solace in age. She was considered stupid, or supposed her family thought her so; extreme nearsightedness made her appear awkward and dull. When she was eleven, she began doggedly to teach herself, and in a few years acquired a reading knowledge of four modern languages. Her English books were those classics which were read by George Eliot, the Brontës, and Margaret Wilson Oliphant; each of these little girls had a special favorite with which the others were not acquainted, and Eliza's was Fox's dolorous *Book of Martyrs*.

At fifteen some kind soul had her fitted with spectacles, which brightened her world considerably, and at seventeen a two-edged compliment roused in her a passion for cleanliness; someone observed that it was a pity such beautiful hair should be so dirty. From a bouncing girl she grew into what the Victorians called "a fine figure of a woman." Her good looks were of a masculine type; experience with her brothers had taught her that it was a fine thing to be a boy; she insisted that she herself had a man's soul—"the top-coating" had been nature's mistake.

In her indignation against her father, she set herself in opposition to his politics and religious principles; because he was a High Tory, she proclaimed herself a Whig—Lafayette and O'Connell were her heroes—and because her father and grandfather were clergymen, she decided, with mingled triumph and terror, that the Virgin Birth was a myth and the Bible a storybook. These rebellious attitudes do not seem in Eliza's case to have been adopted for effect but to have grown out of a strong sense of injustice. Probably her father was less eccentric, the brothers less brutal than she supposed; it was her belief, not the facts, which made her an insurgent.

She was an ambitious girl and a persistent. When at twenty-three she could flourish two guineas paid her for an article in *Ainsworth's Magazine,* she persuaded her father to finance her during a year in London, promising to employ the time in the British Museum, where she planned to write an historical novel. London was the mecca for young career women; within a few years not only Eliza, but

Marian Evans, Margaret Oliphant, and Dinah Mulock would all be writing there, although only well-behaved Dinah Mulock would enjoy absolute independence with a latchkey of her own.

Eliza's father intrusted her to friends of the family, but their kindly restraint was not needed; her determination to prove herself a genius was enough to keep her out of mischief. *Azeth the Egyptian* (1846) won her the nickname of "Miss Sennacherib" and a reputation for appalling erudition. But her early years in London interest us today not because of her somewhat clumsy dealings with the remote past, but because she knew many celebrities in artistic and literary society. She saw much of Thornton Hunt, G. H. Lewes, and their wives and, in John Chapman's boardinghouse, made friends with the untidy and countrified Marian Evans. In later days when Miss Evans turned into "George Eliot," a celebrity to be envied, not patronized, Eliza did not like her in the least. Eliza's recollections are not wholly trustworthy because they are colored by emotion. Mrs. Browning, the poetess, after one of her searching stares at the flinching Miss Lynn, pronounced her "not true," which hurt the girl's feelings and was scarcely fair; Eliza Lynn was true to the feelings of the hour and, like many of us, meant what she wrote while she wrote it.

The susceptibility to beauty in her own sex which made her the champion of Lewes's first wife influenced her marriage to James Linton, the poet and wood engraver, whom she accepted with his six undisciplined children as a legacy from her friend, the lovely, improvident Mrs. Linton. Try as Eliza honestly did to cope with this burdensome ready-made family, she found the situation insupportable. The little Lintons liked her, but, where she was neat, they were incorrigibly untidy: their feet scuffed up the carpets. James Linton too discovered that the marriage was not a success and fled from it to

America, at which safe distance the pair corresponded in a friendly way, although neither was willing to risk a meeting when Linton returned to England.

A very hard worker, Mrs. Lynn Linton wrote a prodigious quantity on the social questions of her day. Our interest, however, is not in the publicist but in the woman who wrote novels.

Azeth the Egyptian, the dry fruit of her year in the British Museum, brought her the friendship of Landor, who was then living in Bath, an exile from Florence and his family of cormorants. The chivalrous old man always liked handsome young girls, but none of the many whose friendship adorned his life was more faithful and kind than Eliza Lynn. She paid him a yearly visit, called him "father," and was well content to hear him say she was his "spiritual daughter." Both had, and deserved, the reputation of being extremely difficult, but they never quarreled with each other.

Amymone (1848), a tale of the times of Pericles, was her second novel. Aspasia, who played an important role, was thickly calcimined, probably because of Landor's influence, but the purification was on the surface and Eliza's Aspasia lacked the nobility of Landor's conception. The vast amount of wickedness in her heroine Amymone and the spirit of revolt which animated the writer did not save the book from being dull and wordy. Eliza's third novel, *Realities,* was so bold in its defiance of convention that John Chapman dared not publish it without revision. Her subject was the contemporary stage, of which she knew nothing personally: George Lewes may have given her material; he would have enjoyed shocking her by relating family experiences in fictionalized form. Hearsay and undigested chunks of book learning were the sources of these early works, but *The Autobiography of Christopher Kirkland* was firmly rooted in her life. The description of rural England in her childhood was equaled rather than surpassed by George Eliot in *Felix Holt the Radical*. Conceiving of herself as the man Christopher, but determined to tell her own story, Eliza inverted the sexes of her other characters, a proceeding which causes some distrust of the psychological validity of her presentation. This bitter human document contains her own absorbing case history.

Gradually Mrs. Lynn Linton's ideas and attitudes became firmly fixed. The scared, little girl skeptic, grown a young woman, accepted Marian Evans's translation of Strauss's *Das Leben Jesu* as confirmation of her doubts. She decided that God did not answer prayer; a God who refused to answer when addressed was clearly not intelligent, and an unintelligent God was of no use to the Universe; therefore, said Eliza, always a practical girl, there is no God. Her theories of sex were equally bold for Victorian times; she believed the institution of marriage too strict and—oddly enough—too monotonous to endure, and saw in the ideal of chastity nothing more significant than the result of care for the race. In practice, however, she was no latitudinarian. She had no sympathy with the "Girl of Today," was horrified at the idea of mixed classes for medical students, and would not lend her support to the founding of Girton College for women. As she settled more deeply in the grooves of her early brave decisions, she used to justify her pronouncements by the oracular "For I have always said." George Meredith invariably rejected her manuscripts because of her "abhorrence of the emancipation of young females from their ancient rules." As Mrs. Lynn Linton grew into old age, her personal asperities softened. Now and then she paid a visit to her childhood home, where she bent down to smell the bed of sweet lavender, or traced with a worn finger the initials she had carved long ago on the bark of the lime tree. She had forgiven her father for his harshness and neglect, and expressed a wish to lie by his side in death. She had become a tired old lady who often sighed because the life of a journalist was very wearing; she employed odd moments in making little presents of penwipers or pincushions for her friends. Eliza had begun as a rebel, but died not only patiently acquiescent in her own destiny, but asking no better fate for those who should come after.

MRS. ARCHER CLIVE is classed among the rebels, not because she willfully obstructed the course of Victorian morals, but because she was unaware of its existence. Miss Mitford, who was too indulgent to be trusted implicitly as a witness, described Mrs. Clive as a woman of great gaiety of heart, but I have been able to discover no one else of her opinion. Mrs. Browning, who met Mrs. Clive in Rome, observed not only that she was a very peculiar person, but that she seemed unaware of her peculiarities, and Crabb Robinson recorded lugubriously that Mrs. Clive was "very, very plain," referring to her appearance, not to the limpidity of her mind. During the Welsh singing festivals, she entertained guests in her palatial country house; we do not know how much the guests saw of their hostess nor what they thought about her.

She had been born in the second year of the century, Caroline Meysey-Wigley, an heiress to great wealth. Before her fourth birthday, an illness crippled her for life. At forty she married the clergyman Archer Clive, and became the mother of a boy and a girl who eventually inherited her estates. It is pleasant hearing that this woman, although a cripple, an invalid, and so "very, very plain," lived "to hold my son's son on my knee."

As Caroline Clive published her first book a year after her marriage, it is reasonable to give her husband the credit of encouraging her talent. The *Quarterly Review* pronounced some of the stanzas in the thin volume with the odd title, *IX Poems by V* (1840), "worthy of anyone of our greatest poets in his happiest moments." The verses are extremely melodious and sorrowful, varying in sentiment from the pensive to the inconsolable. They express her grief at the restrictions which her invalidism placed upon her and her dread lest her character deteriorate under the burden of incessant pain.

The outline of her story resembled that of Elizabeth Barrett Browning, but Mrs. Clive does not seem to have induced or welcomed invalidism. She did not need it as a protection from malign influences and was resentful because it obstructed her talents:

> My fond ambition crush'd ere it could be
> Aught save a self-consuming, wasted fire.

But though she suffered, she did not die and she even managed a fair amount of writing, until in her mid fifties she found herself suddenly famous. Presently the nature of her fame made her very uncomfortable. The wealthy Mrs. Clive, wife of a clergyman, an invalid lady, almost a recluse, was publicly charged with having produced an immoral novel. The *Quarterly Review,* which had so recently praised her poems, asserted that in *Paul Ferroll* she had perversely pictured a criminal as "the mildest, noblest, most humane of men." Sensitive Mrs. Clive protested that she had drawn a character in whom intellect took the place of conscience; she had not expected her readers to approve of her hero. The character has remained an enigma for almost a century: Ferroll is a courteous and refined gentleman with a delicate sense of honor, deeply in love with an innocent and exquisite woman; at the same time he is the perpetrator of a brutal and revolting murder; he is ruthless, cold, friendless, indifferent to the happiness of his attached and charming daughter. In her loneliness and sequestration Mrs. Clive had succumbed to Paul Ferroll's fascination as completely as Charlotte Brontë yielded to her Zamorna. Both women were captivated by the idea of masculine power, but the matron, more fastidious than the spinster, insisted upon elegance and subtlety. She has been wrongly credited with originating the villain as hero; it is more correct to say that few writers have created so well-bred and coolly courteous a monster.

Three years later, Mrs. Clive, who was by this time fifty-seven, published a masterpiece which was not successful at the time and has since lain in obscurity. The story is based on the refusal of an insurance company to pay off a policy. The first half of the book consists of episodes, but the masterly recapitulation in the latter half proves Mrs. Clive a deliberate and skillful plotter. *Year after Year* could not be popular with Victorian readers; the economy of means is too severe, love interest in the usual sense is wanting, the wild and charming brother who might have carried the novel dies too soon, and the narrator, who is his illegitimate half-sister, has little to recommend her but her doglike fidelity. In defiance of these disadvantages, the emotion excited by the girl's heroic effort is so intense as to exhaust the reader, and although *Year after Year* is by no means so audacious and brilliant as *Paul Ferroll*, it would make a much better scenario.

Mrs. Clive had never coveted many days. She had really hated her invalidism and in one of her early poems had thus invoked sudden death:

> With all my wit, my soul, my heart,
> Burning away in every part,
> That so more meetly I might fly
> Into mine immortality;
> Like comets when their race is run,
> That end by rushing on the sun.

Life, with its genius for irony, granted her wish, but not until she was seventy-two years old. She was burned to death in her boudoir, from which her lameness made escape impossible.

THERE ARE VARIETIES among our rebellious novelists. Eliza Lynn Linton was a publicist, Mrs. Clive an exotic; Harriet Martineau was a teacher. Were she not Miss Martineau, we might deny her a place in this chapter, where she has less right than Mrs. Marsh or Geraldine Jewsbury or Fanny Trollope. Three quarters of a century have elapsed since Harriet's death, and she herself assured the world that there was no life beyond the grave. But if she could conceivably be wrong, if her shade lingers on the threshold, it would be wisdom not to contradict her claim to be a novelist. She has a pleasant virtue in that she is one of the few Victorian writers who make no demand on our sympathy. She enjoyed her struggles, her quarrels, and her afflictions. We may marvel at her self-conceit and smile at her absurdities, but her courage and persistence move us to admiration.

Harriet Martineau was born in 1802 in the cathedral city of Norwich, which was then strongly influenced by a group of intellectual Unitarians. As her own family belonged to that enlightened sect, Harriet received an excellent education. In childhood she was, like many little girls, often unhappy; she believed that no one loved her, wished to run away, contemplated suicide, had indigestion, and told her mother lies.

Eliza Lynn Linton, who never knew her mother, grew up believing that if she had lived, her own life would have been happy. Harriet, who knew her mother a long time, did not consider herself privileged. She never understood Mrs. Martineau, never guessed that the preposterous errands on which she sent her daughter, that the scoldings and the dramatic exclamations, afforded the older woman the release which Harriet found in other ways. Mrs. Martineau was not a bad mother; she sat up late to mend Harriet's stockings, provided her with competent teachers, saw to it that she had music lessons, and was even detected in tears when sweetvoiced Harriet was singing in the next room.

Although Harriet as a little girl could sing and play, she never became an accomplished musician because she grew deaf in her earliest teens. At first her mental suffering over her affliction was intense, but, although she was only a child, she had a store of courage and self-confidence and was soon able to treat her limitation as an advantage. For the rest of her long life she sported an ear trumpet. After she became famous, she would carry two of these contrivances to dinner parties, where she would toss one with an extra long tube to the speaker at the opposite end of the table. When his talk bored or offended her, or when she felt that she could finish the sentence better herself—and this was very often—she would snatch back her trumpet.

It was to be expected that a girl brought up in a family of strict Unitarians would begin her literary career by writing for a religious periodical. During her late twenties Harriet won three prizes in a competition concerned with the best methods of presenting Unitari-

anism to Mohammedans, Jews, and Catholics. It is worthy of
record that the Mohammedan price was highest, worth indeed
twenty guineas, while the Jews were rated at fifteen, and the
Catholics at a mere ten. By the time Harriet was thirty, her father
was dead and the family means were exhausted, so that she had an
excellent excuse for shedding Norwich gentility and making what
money she could by writing. Political economy was the fashionable
subject of the hour, and Harriet, who never lacked self-confidence,
determined to present its principles in a series of tales. Her mission
as a teacher of the ignorant would always mean more to her than
money, and her war cry, "the public want this book and they shall
have it," was an expression of genuine and comfortable belief. For
a variety of reasons the *Illustrations of Political Economy* (1832–34)
were phenomenally successful, and Harriet promptly became a
person of importance. She accepted fame as her due and increased
the value of her social appearances by refusing uninteresting invitations and letting it be known that a person who worked for the
public weal could not be expected to make calls.

Her prominence had one disadvantage; convention made it
necessary to have her mother live with her in London. Harriet complained that Mrs. Martineau was jealous because invitations to the
popular daughter did not include the old mother; she accused Mrs
Martineau of being cross because she refused to take a larger house
and live in better style. But she admitted that the poor lady tried to
cost her as little as she could, and, inadvertently, she gives us glimpses
of an astute old woman quietly laying out her treasured pearls for
Harriet to wear to Victoria's coronation, holding the sal volatile to
the publicist's nose while Harriet corrected proofs in her sickbed,
and continually encouraging her daughter in her career. The situa-

tion was peculiarly Victorian; although Harriet and her mother could not agree, they must live together "for the speech of people." The younger woman very properly broke the connection, but in doing so her methods were tortuous, resentment against the old mother lingered, and the daughter felt the necessity of justifying her action. The famous American tour, on which she consorted with Unitarian abolitionists and ran, or supposed she ran, a risk of being hanged in the wilds of Ohio, was largely prompted by the need of a long respite from Mrs. Martineau. After her return, Harriet's illness made a final separation possible. She settled herself happily at Tynemouth with an abdominal tumor, received much company, and wrote a vast amount, including charming stories for children.

Five years later she dismissed her illness and at the same time put an end to the danger of a reconciliation with her mother by the delightful discovery that mesmerism had cured her. From this time she was greatly influenced by Henry Atkinson, a handsome, icy apostle of mesmerism, who convinced her of the folly of those remnants of Christianity which still clung about her. It was her firm belief that her duty to the public involved her publishing her opinions on every subject. With Mr. Atkinson as collaborator, in *Letters on the Laws of Man's Nature and Development* (1851) she announced her abrogation of earlier religious beliefs. This action formed a further bulwark against her mother, who, as a Christian, felt it impossible to make her home with an infidel. Harriet had once very tenderly loved her brother James, the famous Unitarian preacher and philosopher, but when this affection interfered with the way of life she had chosen, she repudiated him.

Ten cheerful, productive years passed in her charming house in Ambleside. Then, in her early fifties, she felt a recurrence of old symptoms and, going to town, consulted two London physicians. She was told that the pain arose from the abdominal tumor; mesmerism had not cured it, but at the time of the supposed healing, the growth had shifted to a position where it ceased to trouble her; it had now, unfortunately, moved again. Whether this diagnosis possessed any scientific value is of no importance to us; it is the effect it had on Miss Martineau in which we are interested. It placed her in the most awkward of positions: if she repeated the physicians' opinion to her friends, she would discredit her friend Atkinson and mesmerism and, worse, admit that she was not infallible. After brief consideration, she determined to suppress the diagnosis; she announced that she was about to die from heart disease.

Twenty-one years of genial dying followed. She wrote her bequest to the public, the *Autobiography* (published 1877), and laid it aside. Her life was very busy, very cheerful. The docile among her relations, friends, neighbors were subject to her improving methods; no one was left who dared interfere with her. Nor did anyone hint that the hourly awaited demise was long in coming; the delightful old autocrat had never been more popular than in these years of pleasant invalidism. Because of her political principles, she refused a Crown pension three times offered her, thinking perhaps of Caesar, but she accepted a fund of £1400 raised by private subscription. Thirteen hundred pounds were invested in an annuity, but the irrespressible Harriet disgusted Mr. Wedgwood and Mr. Darwin, who had engineered the collection of funds, by asking that the remainder be spent on silver—she had been studying a jeweler's catalogue and coveted a certain handsome teapot.

Her novel *Deerbrook* (1839) had been written in her late thirties. It was didactic but not dull, a tale of an English village in which superstition, jealousy, gossip, ignorance, poverty, and cholera threatened the loves of two Birmingham sisters. Harriet's own love idyll had been of the slightest; the only passions she could understand were those of bad temper and a desire to get on in the world. Nor did she show any remarkable powers of characterization, being especially inept in her masculine types: the gentlemen in business together might have been identical twins; the lovers, blood brothers.

It had been necessary in her *Illustrations* to cope with the question of sex in marriage and with the doctrines of Malthus. She explained that she had done this without offense because she had treated it from a purely philosophical standpoint. The result could not be described as practical. She too was not a believer in Women's Rights, though it seemed odd to her that Miss Martineau had no vote; however, she believed that women would obtain equal rights with men when they had been educated to deserve them. She had in turn proclaimed herself an abolitionist, a believer in mesmerism, and an infidel. The Victorians had shown brief wonder at these startling pronouncements, but had allowed her to go on lecturing them. Had she lived in our own times, the fine tart flavor of her individuality might have been wanting, and the world would have been the loser.

THE WOMEN THUS FAR CONSIDERED were not peculiarly unfortunate, although they were unable to conform to the dictates of popular opinion. A fourth novelist, Catherine Crowe, was much more to be pitied, not because of Victorian injustices, but because of mental instability. She was probably born in 1800 and died in 1876, thus being an almost exact contemporary of Caroline Clive and Harriet Martineau. We know little of her private life. She was born Catherine Stevens, married at twenty-two, lived many years in Edinburgh, moved to London, where she was mentioned without comment as a guest at many literary parties—including that unsocial gathering at Thackeray's house in honor of Charlotte Brontë. During her fifties she became insane and was arrested because of eccentricities which "the spirits" had recommended; she was taken before a London magistrate and confined in a jail from which it is to be hoped her friends immediately removed her. Her intense preoccupation with the supernatural may have resulted from a morbid condition or may have produced it; she believed in ghosts, studied German sources, made a magnificent collection of ghost stories, and wrote a treatise on spiritualism. After she recovered her wits, she confined herself largely to children's stories.

Superstition was too rampant in the fifties and sixties for the poor woman's belief in spirits to be accepted as a sign of insanity. Nor was the fact that she was a disciple of George Combe, the phrenologist, any indication of disease when so many level-headed folk had confidence in this refinement of fortune-telling. Perhaps her entire want of humor influenced her fate. Students of the occult can place little reliance in a scientific sense in her treasure house of tales of the supernatural, *The Night Side of Nature* (1848), because she accepted without investigation whatever wild stories were offered her; and yet it is not worthless even to those who do not borrow plots. Her explanation of forgotten dreams, her apprehension of the subconscious, and acceptance of the theory that the past is always with us possess potential value. The modern mind is moved to speculative pity over the poor woman who found the Victorian arena so bare that she must people it with shadows from the underworld.

The *Adventures of Susan Hopley* (1841) was published when she was forty-one, a book of the mid-century, although the flavor of the delightful adventure story is that of Smollett's time. Astounding incidents were retailed with an extraordinary realism. Coincidences abounded, and too often an understanding of events depended upon what was overheard; yet there was nothing vulgar, as in the prying of Mrs. Henry Wood's sub-heroine Barbara, in *East Lynne* (1861), or indeed among Henry James's ill-mannered house guests. Mrs. Crowe's credulity was not that of Defoe, since hers was real and his assumed for literary purposes; she would have thought it sin to doubt the ghost of Mrs. Veal. Mrs. Carlyle, who knew Mrs. Crowe slightly, observed that her own life was sometimes very like that lady's novels—"futile in the extreme, but so full of plot that the *interest* has never been allowed to flag"; and this is much the impression *Susan Hopley* makes upon the modern reader.

ONE MORE SOCIETY REBEL, and we shall go on to ladies of propriety. The beautiful Caroline Norton, granddaughter of the great Sheridan, was the most picturesque of the century's rebellious lady novelists, and might have posed for a statue symbolic of the victim of unjust marriage laws. When she was nineteen, her relations passed her on to the lazy, unamiable, and brutal George Norton, who made her a thoroughly bad husband. She was too handsome, too conspicuous not to be remarked, and before she had been married a year had become the subject of gossip because of her visits to her literary adviser, Harrison Ainsworth, with whose help she published, at twenty, her first slim volume of poetry.

Probably she was never guilty of anything worse than frantic rashness. The two chief accusations brought against her, her relations with Lord Melbourne and the alleged sale of a state secret to *The Times,* were certainly without foundation. George Meredith, who made a perverted use of her history in *Diana of the Crossways*, ungallantly protested that he had endowed his heroine with brains. But it was not brains which Caroline Norton lacked, it was good sense. In her marital relations she quarreled too easily with her husband and forgave him much too easily. When they separated, although he was the guilty party, the law granted him the custody of their little boys to whom she was passionately attached. They were neglected, and one died of lockjaw after an accident with his pony.

The intrepid mother fought her husband in and out of the courts; she wrote pamphlets, exhausted her friends' patience, and, although she had right on her side, became that Victorian horror, a notorious female. Indirectly her fusillade helped to better the laws relating to infant custody, while her shocking misfortunes, forced upon public notice, gradually softened the attitude of society toward women placed in such invidious positions.

Her beauty was very great, and her poems are evocative of the woman who wrote them. "Juanita," which she composed for her son to sing to his guitar, suggests her husky sweetness; "The King of Denmark's Ride" is chivalrous; there is fine sentiment in "The Lady of La Garaye." She worked harder than anyone could have expected, and was a constant contributor to such elegant publications as *The Keepsake, The Book of Beauty,* and *Friendship's Offering,* earning at one period as much as £1400 a year. Yet to her distress she was always considered a gifted amateur. When Samuel Rogers mentioned her as the author of "fugitive pieces," she lay long awake fancying herself surrounded by the white slips of paper on which she had penned her verses; how mockingly they bowed to her, with what malignancy chanted, "We are Fugitive Pieces"!

Her trials never toughened her against criticism. She was furious when her poems were stolen or were attributed to other authors. She was afraid that her sons would be alienated from her by her husband's family. Her life was the more unfortunate because she was peculiarly unfit to stand alone, and few of the prudent dared stand beside her. In her old age, long after George Norton's death, she married Sir William Stirling-Maxwell, but died three months later.

Her only noteworthy novel, *Stuart of Dunleath* (1851), was a fictionized version of her wretched marriage, but the violent Sir Stephen Penrhyn is treated with a sympathy which makes her frequent reconciliations with George Norton less difficult to understand; his brutal strength must have appealed to the tempestuous girl. Her mournful words on women who leave their husbands rang in the ears of many an unhappy Victorian wife: "They must have friends, home, money, a protection of some sort, somewhere to go." An incident in *Stuart of Dunleath* reveals a dark pocket of Victorian morality: the heroine refuses her husband a divorce, alleging a determination to save her soul by preserving her marriage—although she will not live with him—a decision which prevents her husband's marriage to his mistress and works harm to his innocent, illegitimate children: thus egoism and a wish for vengeance are cloaked as virtues. The novel was published in 1851. A quarter of a century later *Daniel Deronda* dealt with a similar problem from a higher ethical standpoint, but the difference lay less in the passage of time than in the women who wrote the books. Mrs. Norton was a lovely egoist; George Eliot was able to treat the case of Grandcourt, Lydia Glasher, and Gwendolen objectively.

Caroline Norton endured her misfortunes with unquenchable spirit. She suffered and recovered. Nor can all her griefs be attributed to a bad husband and injurious laws; women of her stamp do not lead tranquil lives. Her charming if slender talents, her peerless beauty, and her tragic misfortunes make her perhaps the most brilliant female figure of the century.

ALTHOUGH SUCH LADIES found cold comfort in the Procrustean bed of propriety, there were many writers to whom the conditions imposed by society were anything but grievous. In every period the sentimentalist in letters has the knack of keeping within the barriers erected by the opinion of her public. When we speak of sentimentalists, we refer to those writers who exaggerated the emotions which they recognized and ignored or misrepresented those to which they were unfavorable in order to present a fictitious picture of life.

The always moral, always trite Mrs. Gore (1800–1861) exerted royal authority over English readers by a combination of inflexible standards of behavior and a knowledge of aristocratic circles. Where she learned so much about the upper classes is a matter of conjecture; she was born into a mercantile family, but seems to have been the stepdaughter of a Dr. Nevinson; at twenty-three she married Lieutenant Charles Arthur Gore, who retired almost immediately from the army and subsequently assisted her in the writing of plays and novels. They lived some years in France and in Belgium, where he died in 1846. In the intervals of bearing him ten children, she had published a staggering number of volumes; before her own death at sixty-one, she had produced fifty-five works of fiction.

Miss Mitford had known her as a young girl and considered her a most brilliant conversationalist. She was undoubtedly an accomplished woman, an excellent musician, the composer of drawing-room songs. The outline of her life is bleak enough: she was left a widow at forty-six; at fifty she inherited a fortune, only to be cheated out of most of it; she became blind and ceased either to go out or to receive visitors; of her ten children only two survived her.

Mrs. Gore's six years in France did not alter her insular opinions of the French nation; the Revolution, Bonaparte, and the heartless frivolity of the French people were all abhorrent to her. One of her characters, Lady Mereworth, a perfectly proper British matron nearing forty, is completely demoralized by a four months' visit to Paris. Yet Mrs. Gore, like Mrs. Trollope, admitted the superior taste and grace of French women: "The ambition of a French beauty is to be *'belle parmi les belles'*—of an English beauty, to make other women look ugly." This harmless inset in the quotation leads us to consider one of Mrs. Gore's most annoying idiosyncrasies. George Eliot, who was herself no mean pedant, probably had her in mind when she savagely attacked lady novelists for parading their acquaintance with foreign languages. Mrs. Gore was a chief offender. Her readers, most of whom belonged to the upper classes, could make out her French; but her Latin and Greek and the occasional German printed in big black Gothic letters must have impressed rather than enlightened her feminine public.

Besides this troublesome peculiarity stands Mrs. Gore's addiction to long words; her meaning lies concealed in polysyllables, and the tiny kernel when extracted is no such great matter. It may well be that neither her quotations nor her circumlocution were intended primarily to impress her readers; it seems rather as if unconsciously she attempted to conceal herself and her private feelings from a world for which she had no very warm sentiments. We are not likely to find out the truth about Mrs. Gore, and this impression of a sensitive, fugitive spirit, of a clever woman who did not very much like to write but was forced into it, is as authentic as any.

Clever she undoubtedly was. The bitter wit of *Cecil a Peer,* written in her early middle age, and the authority with which she treats of social history in England and France in the late twenties and the thirties make it quite understandable that intelligent people were her devoted readers. Cecil Danby, formerly a "coxcomb," is prone to take a sentimental view which, on reflection, stiffens into hardheartedness, although he is honestly attached to his elder brother. There is no plot and only one bit of worth-while characterization, that of a doctor who is clearly limned in a matter of two pages, an instance of the excellent portrayal of minor figures by Victorian novelists. But Mrs. Gore was looking back upon well-remembered events, and her relation of extraordinary attitudes over the Catholic and Reform Bills, the coronation of William IV—many diarists recorded that of Victoria, but how few troubled themselves with the Sailor King's!—and the selfish efforts of society to improve the conditions of the masses in order to keep back the cholera from the classes, atones for the puerility of the figures which appear upon her stage. Instead of being a mother of numerous children and of many insipid novels Mrs. Gore should have been a Victorian gentleman and a historian.

George IV praised her *Women as They Are; or, The Manners of the Day* (1830) as "the best-bred and most amusing novel he had ever read." It is charming to learn how readily His Majesty was entertained, for the story seems to us excessively dull. Echoes of life in London clubs, on great estates in Ireland, a duel, balls at Almack's, pursuit of virtuous ladies by gentlemen who mean them no good—how can a book be dull in which such exciting events occur? But there is no life in Mrs. Gore's novels, merely cold propriety and colder vice. Yet she knew her times and adequately presented the delights and dangers of the fashionable world. The innocent flirtations of childish wives, sold by their families to middle-aged diplomats who will not spare time to look after their little purchases, are rendered fearfully hazardous by gossip. To these girls sex seems merely an odd inconvenience incidental to their new existence; Mrs. Gore's discretion does not permit a nearer view.

The Dean's Daughter; or, The Days We Live In (1853) was written almost a quarter of a century after *Women as They Are,* but the veteran novelist had not improved with the years. The only clever bit of characterization—that of the valetudinarian Dean—was apparently borrowed from Jane Austen's Mr. Woodhouse: Mrs. Gore believed herself a Jane Austen in high life. Students of society in the fifties may learn something of those principles by which discreet young women were expected to regulate their conduct: men will always talk women over, therefore young women must be extraordinarily careful not to provide food for gossip at the clubs; it is not safe for a woman to act independently even in trifles; to marry without love is an error, but love must not be given unasked, and love itself must be untouched by carnal desire; if a woman yields her virtue to a lover without becoming aware of his physical attraction, she may be pardoned—after her death; if she has yielded through passion, she will be neither mourned nor forgiven.

The Dean's daughter violated a cardinal principle—she married without love—and had a dull life of it until an early suitor reappeared and half-heartedly undertook to seduce her. No sooner had she determined to yield than he somewhat ungallantly announced his approaching marriage to another lady. Saved in spite of herself, the Dean's daughter vowed to expiate her brief aberration by devoting her life to her excellent, if prosy, husband. But Mrs. Gore would not let her off with this easy repentance; she contrived a railway accident to kill the husband, cripple the heir, and render the vacillating heroine wretched for life. Her readers were spared the horror of suspecting that passion caused the original breach of decorum: "It was no frailty of the senses which was obtaining dominion over her. It was the foolish romance of false sentiment,—the upstarting of a long-smouldering first love, imperfectly extinguished in her girlhood."

A languid elegance, a flow of fine language, the confidence of social "tone" recommended Mrs. Gore to her public; she "opened to us the glittering doors of the aristocracy and made us free of the Exclusives," said Eliza Lynn Linton, while Mrs. Oliphant, who was much too clever to enjoy Mrs. Gore's novels as novels, professed to hear the rustle of rich silks and the frou-frou of velvets sweep along the printed page.

SENTIMENTAL NOVELS are confined to no period and differ surprisingly little in treatment, subject, and style from one generation to another. They are properly domestic, although the marriage finale was less common in the last century than today, when the Sweet and Simple chronicles almost invariably close just this side of the altar. Among Victorian sentimentalists Dinah Maria Mulock Craik was preëminent in talent.

Her simple history accounts for the quality of her work. Her father was a handsome, eccentric Irishman who became a Baptist preacher and removed from one small charge to another, sometimes to none, so that her girlhood was insecure and she received little schooling but was herself a teacher at thirteen in a class managed by her mother. She grew up tall, slender—what the Victorians called "willowy"—a very pretty girl with a soulful gaze and the friendly manner appropriate to a minister's daughter. Like Eliza Lynn Linton, she yearned for London as the promised land. In 1840 the family moved to the metropolis and a few years later, Dinah, in her early twenties, had become the center of a literary and artistic group. To have an English version of the *salon* was every writing woman's ambition; the gatherings in Dinah Mulock's Hampstead cottage were as cheerful as they were second-rate. She was an excellent business woman and knew how to get the most money from her books; Mrs. Oliphant reported that Hurst the publisher used to turn pale when he spoke of Miss Mulock's bargaining powers. When she married it was into the business; her husband, the crippled Mr. Craik, ten years her junior, was a partner of her friend, Alexander Macmillan.

She loved children and adopted a little daughter, whom she named Dorothy—the gift of God. Mrs. Craik wrote touchingly sentimental poems on childhood as well as those two excellent and still much read juveniles, *The Adventures of a Brownie* (1872) and *The Little Lame Prince* (1875). As she grew older and her interest in her characters faded, she tried to replace her lost freshness by pious admonitions. In many ways the busy, kindly, saving woman remained a little girl; she had neither time nor inclination to study; Renan's *Life of Christ* horrified her into a decision that all she could do was blindly trust and hold fast the beliefs of childhood. Her trade was the writing of love stories, and she enjoyed the position she held in the respect of Evangelical wives and mothers. She built a fine house on the proceeds of her books, and, in spite of criticism, accepted a pension from the crown which she did not in the least need.

Her only important novel, *John Halifax, Gentleman* (1856), is the life story of a good man, to whom integrity, intelligence, and industry bring success. A certain breadth of view is shown in the realistic treatment of the second generation, who develop in opposition to the wishes of the parents but tend in maturity to return to the family pattern. Mrs. Craik liked the first-person narrative, a device which is successful only with the most skillful writers. The narrator of *John Halifax, Gentleman* is a crippled Quaker, Jonathan to the David of the knightly hero. John Halifax's innocent snobbery arises from his sole inheritance, a little New Testament inscribed with his father's name followed by the word *Gentleman*. This relic not unnaturally inspires him to shape his life after the Victorian ideal and become a Gentleman himself. The book is uncommonly interesting as a chronicle of the first half of the century. John Halifax is a tanner, a millowner, master of men, an innovator with machinery; he has vaccinated his children, stopped a run on the bank, ousted the wicked lord's candidate in a parliamentary election. He may seem too pious, too uxorious for modern taste; his virtues are Arthurian; he may be a British replica of the Prince Consort, but he deserves respect, even applause.

Mrs. Craik wrote many other novels, all of them very bad. Her first, *The Ogilvies* (1849) was a silly book; Mrs. Carlyle called it "full of love as an egg is of meat—old, highflown romantic Circulating Library sort of Love." Yet Miss Mitford could be convinced that the author of this foolish tale was her adored Mrs. Browning. Twenty years later, *The Woman's Kingdom*, and thirty years later, *Young Mrs. Jardine,* were no less puerile. Mrs. Craik's own favorite, *A Life for a Life* (1859), was a preposterous hodgepodge of slaying, coincidence, fidelity, persecution, with an old Oedipus in the background, a ministerial father, apparently modeled on Mr. Brontë as he had been portrayed in the recently published biography of Charlotte Brontë. Mrs. Craik was also indebted to Charlotte Brontë for her small, plain, pale heroines and for her bold assertion that a woman might decently love before she knew her love returned, although she did not go to the Brontë length of permitting her heroine to confess her passion. Indeed her novels of contemporary life were hedged about with propriety; two brothers who had spent a summer in the same lodginghouse with twin sisters could not, without impertinence, inquire the girls' London address; even under harrowing anxiety a young man might not enter a young lady's sitting room without first summoning the landlady to chaperon him. Yet this wearisome etiquette is less annoying than Mrs. Craik's personal piety. We might forgive her characters their spiritual soliloquies and prayers, but we cannot forgive her own interpolations, her frequent reminders of "One" who sits above, her growing dependence on exhortation. In spite of her humbug, her effervescence and shallowness, *John Halifax, Gentleman* entitles her to fifth place among women novelists of the century, directly after the four great writers, Charlotte Brontë, Elizabeth Gaskell, George Eliot, and Mrs. Oliphant.

BUT WHILE WE EXPRESS leniency for Mrs. Craik's shortcomings because we believe them due to early disadvantages, there rises before us the inconvenient phenomenon of our third sentimental novelist, Mrs. Henry Wood, over whose nursery good fairies presided, whose childhood was blessed by every influence of wealth and culture.

The grandmother with whom Ellen Price Wood spent her infancy belonged to a "county" family; Ellen's father had been educated for the Church, but had chosen the career of a "simple manufacturer." The arduous business of glovemaking was not, however, permitted to engross his leisure; he spent his days in his study with his small daughter at his side, while he read the classics, amused himself with water colors, or solaced incipient ennui by making music. His ruffles were snowy, his manners exquisite. Ellen's mother, although less elegant, was saved from mediocrity by her happy faculty of seeing ghosts. The enormous house of the fabulously wealthy Prices stood hard by Worcester Cathedral. Little Ellen was wont to roam the cloisters, reflecting, she has informed us, upon "the happy dead." The social circle of the family was that of the dignitaries of the Church, whom, from her earliest years, the artless Ellen entertained with recitations.

As she entered her teens, a curvature of the spine made itself apparent. Four years later a fixation of the vertebrae occurred; already deformed and crippled, she grew no worse. The young girl exhibited a surprising strength of mind. She did not flourish her defects as Harriet Martineau did her ear trumpet, but refused to acknowledge them. She studied out a dress which concealed to some extent the distortion of her figure, practiced a graceful walk, and determined not to give up dancing. Although she was always frail and, as a lady should, encouraged the reputation of genteel delicacy, she married young and bore several healthy children. Twenty years were passed with her husband in France. He is known only by his admiration for "Henry Wood's lady"; we learn that he used to carry her out of their magnificent château to their own carriage drawn by four horses, when they set out on one of their frequent visits to those

French aristocrats who acclaimed Mrs. Wood in her "flowing, white, and airy material as a creature all romance and imagination."

This halcyon life ended with the loss of her father's money. The middle-aged Mrs. Wood, like Mrs. Trollope, retrieved the family's fortune by writing novels. We should have expected from this delicately nurtured, highly educated lady either an exotic romance or a psychological work such as Mrs. Clive's, whose circumstances were outwardly much like her own; but Mrs. Wood, although nurtured by the best of clerical England, the finest of provincial France, became spontaneously the favorite novelist of ladies' maids, servant girls, and shopkeepers' daughters. Her language and her taste were those of the lower middle class. She was not superior, and never dreamed that superiority was expected of her; there was nothing patronizing in her writing as in the infuriating tones of George Eliot. The lower the walk in life, the more at home Mrs. Wood felt. She peered with her heroines out of windows, crouched beside them at keyholes. The intimacy of her style is that of a crony gossiping at the fireside: "Talk of her having looked ill, you should have seen her now"; while of that dramatic instant when the hero of *East Lynne* realizes that his children's governess is actually the wife who left him for another, Mrs. Wood wrote glibly, "The first clear thought that came thumping through his brain was that he must be a man of two wives."

She could not be described as a widely read woman, although she confessed herself not opposed to a little of Tennyson, a little of Mrs. Browning, less of Byron. Of Longfellow she said approvingly, "In his peculiar way he is very human and adapts himself to quotation." But after her own works were in print, she ceased to regard lesser lights; her novels were precisely suited to her own taste and she never wearied of rereading them. There is something at once touching and comical in the picture of this elegant little invalid, snug in "the prettiest sittingroom in London," arrayed in Lyons silk woven specially to her order, absorbed in reading her own novel.

She made a great deal of money, but as she had been brought up to take wealth as a matter of course, she valued her gains principally as a mark of her public's approbation. She was a conservative in politics and a Churchwoman; she did not think society needed to be reformed, and said she had no doubt that inequality of classes was "Divinely ordered." Respectable publications such as *The Quiver* and *The Leisure Hour* valued her as a contributor, and she and her son, who was her partner and biographer, founded their own magazine—*The Argosy*.

When we contrast Mrs. Craik, who had no education, with Mrs. Wood, who had much more than she could use, we may surmise that environment and education are not of first importance for the writer who adopts an unrealistic attitude toward life. This is not altogether because the readers of sentimental fiction are less exacting. They have their requirements. But the pseudo-romancist has withdrawn from reality into the dream world—not a private dream world like the Brontës', but one accessible to the vulgar. Many such writers lived for months at a time in these luxurious realms of fancy, emerging on occasion to drive a hard bargain with a publisher. The success of Mrs. Craik and Mrs. Wood was largely due to their dream world's being a communal possibility.

ALTHOUGH THE PSEUDO-ROMANCISTS of the century outnumbered all other types of women writers, we shall content ourselves with these three examples, and go on to the consideration of Amelia Ann

Blandford Edwards, who was neither feminist, publicist, tragic wife, nor sentimental authoress, but a business woman who wrote for an honest living.

Her father had been an army officer in the Napoleonic wars but was not of the military caste, having come from a superior farming family. Amelia was an only child and "privately educated," an expression which usually means no education, or such painful self-teaching as Eliza Lynn Linton inflicted upon herself. But Amelia had a bright mother who did her best to make her daughter into an infant prodigy. She was really an extraordinarily gifted little girl who could draw as soon as her fingers were strong enough to clutch a pencil, could read, sing, pick out tunes on the piano, and recite original jingles. At the age of seven, she saw her first verses, "The Knights of Old," published in a penny paper.

When she entered her teens, she became aware of the precarious state of the family finances. A strong, steady desire to make something of herself induced her to become apprenticed to a competent musician for a period of seven years, during which she devoted all her energies to the study of voice, piano, organ, harmony, and composition. At twenty-two she was a handsome young woman with a good presence, a church organist, possessor of a voice which promised success in concert or opera—although she was half inclined to become a painter because she drew exceptionally well and had a feeling for color and form. Had she been rich, she might have had a pleasant, busily idle life; but she had herself to support, and her father and mother already needed assistance. She decided that the surest way for a well-bred girl to earn a living was by the pen.

Those who knew her spoke of the long career on which she now entered as a life of bondage; it was certainly not what she would have chosen if the first requisite of any course had not been its power to provide a livelihood. But she would probably have been equally unfortunate in the musical profession or on the stage, where amateur theatricals had given her reason to think she might be successful. The gods do not shower so many gifts upon their real favorites; Amelia, who found a difficulty in choosing between those with which she knew they had dowered her could have no conception of the existence of her real talent: she was a born archeologist.

Superficially her life as a literary woman resembled Eliza Lynn Linton's, although Miss Edwards had none of that feminist's early turbulence. She was a self-controlled, poised, uncomplaining woman who did her work in a competent, unaffected fashion. She produced eight novels, on each of which she spent two years, grinding them out in the intervals allowed by her commitments to periodicals. She wrote leaders for *The Times,* the *Morning Post,* the *Saturday Review;* her critical notes on art, music, and the drama were exceptionally able, and she had the distinction of never reviewing a book which she had not scrupulously read. Most of her writing was done at night, because she found it easier to work when the house was quiet. In her unpretentious way, she was as businesslike as Anthony Trollope. She reckoned that a *Times* article required an entire night's work, but one for a less exacting public could be finished by three in the morning.

In the 1850's, when she began to write novels, the sensational romance was in vogue. Amelia Edwards, who wrote for money, joined the romancists and conceived loose plots which employed the familiar devices of the secret, the escape, the far journey, preferably to Germany or Italy. Her knowledge of the studio and the stage was a great asset; she was admirable in her descriptions of nature and eminent in the matter of ancient dwellings. The silly romanticism of *Barbara's History* (1864) carried it through many editions, but unconscientious readers skipped the excellent sections on travel, archeology, and history.

Her last novel, *Lord Brackenbury* (1880), went through fifteen editions. It commences with a thrill—an English peer has disappeared and £31,000 worth of diamonds is missing—but almost at once the interest wanes. Miss Edwards has ceased to care what becomes of her earl or of his jewels. But when she describes the eruption of Vesuvius which she had witnessed in 1872, or glowingly details the architecture of Old Morton, the ruined Cheshire manor house named Langtry Grange in the novel, it becomes evident that she cares more for nature than for man, more for the past than the present. Her characterizations were passable because she created uncomplicated figures; she lacked the essential interest of the novelist, the one irreplaceable requisite, an affectionate curiosity concerning men and women.

She was more ingenious as a short story writer because plotting appealed to her scientific mind, and the tale was not long enough to bore her. Although she had not the slightest faith in the supernatural, the ghost stories she furnished for the Christmas numbers of *Household Words* and *All the Year Round* were remarkably realistic. Her "Four Fifteen Express" is still deservedly popular. She could be delicate and even tender; the novelette "Monsieur Maurice" is a sensitive story of a mysterious prisoner. Miss Edwards disciplined herself into what was, for the purposes of her work, an admirable manner. As if conscious that she failed her public through her indifference to character, she made every effort to supply well-written books. "I study style like a poet," she boasted, "calculating even the play of vowel sounds and the music of periods. Style is an instrument which I have practiced sedulously."

When she was a little girl, she could not decide whether she loved better the *Arabian Nights* or Williamson's *Manners and Customs of the Egyptians*. In her early forties, the hard-working woman took an Egyptian holiday which settled the question of favorites and altered the remainder of her life. She fell in love with Egyptian antiquity. From that time she wrote, lectured, really lived for the cause of scientific exploration.

There may be living a few old people who saw Miss Edwards on her triumphal lecture tour of the United States (1889–1890) during which she collected three honorary degrees. This was the close of her career because an accident and the subsequent shock were prelude to her death two years later. She had never married, and it pleased her to bequeath her little property to the cause of Egyptology, of which she had become enamored. In spirit Amelia Edwards was the most modern of the women in this book. Although her power of adjustment to circumstances made her useful and not actively unhappy, she would have been more effective had she belonged to our own times.

WE HAVE MENTIONED the existence of literary partnerships in the century and have already instanced that of Captain and Mrs. Gore, and of Mrs. Henry Wood and her son, coeditors and proprietors of *The Argosy*. Mrs. Trollope and her eldest son, T. Adolphus, present a familiar example; Mrs. Gaskell, who began her brilliant career by collaborating with her husband in a poem, never ceased to draw upon his knowledge of dialect and source materials; all the world

knows of George Eliot's indebtedness to Mr. Lewes. Of such literary partnerships, examples had long since been furnished by the
Halls and the Howitts.

Anna Maria Hall, who was born in 1800, in the same year as
Mrs. Gore and Catherine Crowe, and lived until 1880, was a very
able woman, author of several successful plays and excellent novels
besides many short sketches and fairy tales. *Marian; or, A Young
Maid's Fortunes* (1840), the story of a foundling, is full of incident
and humor: the real heroine is Katty Macane, an inimitable Irish
cook. Mrs. Hall belonged to the coterie of the Howitts and Miss
Mulock; she too had a salon where her unctuous Samuel, Dickens's
"Pecksniff," acted showman as, many years later George Lewes
would do for George Eliot. Her pretty house was called the Rosery,
which, because of Mr. Hall's behavior, was privately corrupted to
"The Roguery." Mrs. Hall was a handsome, stately woman, gracious to her guests, but apparently not much gratified by the flattery
showered upon her. She abhorred Women's Rights, but was zealous
in plans for the succor of prostitutes and street musicians. She had
no children, but had her responsibilities; her mother lived to a great
age in her house.

Although the Halls were hard workers, they were never able to
gain a stable prosperity; a Queen's pension, an annuity bought from
the contributions of their friends, eked out their earnings. Mrs. Hall
believed firmly that every problem of life could be solved by the
spirit of love, but she was not a sentimentalist, and it is from her
that we have borrowed the shrewd pronouncement which heads this
chapter: "Those who would seek to know the *cause* of the *feelings*
and *actions* of men and women must go back to childhood and its
impressions."

Her friend Mary Howitt had a similar horror of Women's Rights but, as the wife of the impractical Pre-Raphaelite William Howitt, understood the importance of her earnings and was an active worker for the Married Women's Property Bill. A century ago, her poetry was esteemed worthy to rank with Keats; a volume was published in which her verses occupied one third, the remainder being divided between those of Keats and the erudite Dean Milman. It is fair to add that this arrangement was made in Philadelphia. One of her novels, *The Heir of Wast-Wayland* (1847), is a delightful story of the Dales folk of Wales, well worth reading as an authentic reflection of life in cottage and hall.

Mary Howitt was unassuming and kind and, except in her middle years when the craze of spiritualism absorbed her, a sensible body. She began life as a Quaker, but ended in the Roman Catholic communion, living very happily in Italy with a charming chapel fitted up in her own house, a benignant confessor, and a devoted daughter to attend her.

It was her goodness, not her industry, which brought her late security. Of the women considered in this chapter only the sentimentalists Mrs. Craik and Mrs. Henry Wood were outstanding business successes. Miss Edwards supported herself in quiet dignity. The others, if they lacked private means, worried along, hoping some day to be granted a pension from the crown; the usual allowance of £100 per annum was a wonderful sweetener of old age.

THE BRILLIANT REBEL, Caroline Norton, clung through her distresses to the prefix "Honorable." Two other Victorian ladies who belonged to the British aristocracy wrote sufficiently well to deserve space in this chapter. The Honorable Emily Lawless, daughter of

Lord Cloncurry, was a prolific and gifted writer of the latter part of Victoria's reign. Her viewpoint was naturally that of the privileged class, and she was unconscious of snobbery when she saved the heroine of *A Chelsea Householder* (1883) from the vulgarity of descent from tenant farmers on the mother's side by granting her blue blood on the paternal. Miss Lawless, whose mother was a dear friend of Margaret Oliphant, never married. She lived into our century, and her hobbies were not those of ordinary Victorians but are listed as "dredging, mothing, gardening, and geologizing."

That we are not concerned with women as poets seems invidious in the case of Emily Lawless, because she was at her finest in verse. Her themes were Eire and Nature, and in Nature she took the dual interest of scientist and worshiper. Her songs and ballads of the Burren, that wild, hilly region of north Clare which hugs the bay of Galway, reveal the most intimate familiarity with the terrain and its legends. But, as Samuel Johnson found out long ago, scientific knowledge often betrays the storyteller, and the light-hearted reader of Lawless novels may sigh over the author's excessive interest in natural phenomena. If *Hurrish: a Study* (1886) should be criticized by the implication of the title, the success of its thesis must be admitted; Miss Lawless has studied; she has concentrated on a narrow region and its inhabitants; the work is properly brief, the descriptions veracious and poetic. But if *Hurrish* is to be judged as a novel, its trickle of life is too slow and the characters are reduced to a handful of promising specimens which Miss Lawless studies through a microscope—with the kindest feelings imaginable. Nor does the ending of the delicate, poetical *Hurrish* please us: the hero escapes the gallows only to be wantonly slaughtered by the author.

The Victorian convention demanded a tragic ending to a serious piece of work; this is one of the reasons why their contemporaries undervalued the novels of Trollope and Margaret Oliphant. But very few authors have the power to create inherently tragic characters, and when destiny sports cruelly with the weak, the spectacle is piteous rather than tragic. The end of the novel is the point at which the author takes leave of his subject, and when the narrative has dealt with simple folk it is wise to say farewell to them while hope remains. Turgenev knew very well when he had finished a story.

The Honorable Emily Eden published only two novels, the first in 1859, when she was sixty-two years old, seven years older than Caroline Clive had been at the issue of her first novel. Chapman and Hall offered Miss Eden £250 for *The Semi-Detached House* (1859), but she anxiously insisted upon £300, a sum on which she had determined because she knew someone else who needed it. The story is cheerful and conventional; the reader learns how very kind aristocrats are to deserving middle-class people. A far better novel succeeded this—*The Semi-Attached Couple* (1860), which she had begun a generation earlier and reworked for publication after her little triumph. Without a doubt Jane Austen inspired *The Semi-Attached Couple,* but the work has independent merit, and when compared to Mrs. Gore's *Women as They Are,* which deals with the same period, it positively scintillates. In one regard Miss Eden is actually superior to Jane Austen, for her servants are better done; a letter from a lady's maid is worthy to be set beside Mr. Collins's immortal epistle. The reader of these two books may well feel that it would be an excellent idea for more women to write novels at thirty and lock them in their desks, to be rewritten when they themselves are sixty.

In our "Ladies' Miscellany," Amelia Edwards, Harriet Martineau, Emily Eden, and Emily Lawless were spinsters; among the matrons Mrs. Craik, Mrs. Lynn Linton, and Mrs. Hall had no children of their own. It seems unlikely that any of them except Amelia Edwards could have supported herself by any means except writing; Mrs. Gore's musical ability is unsupported tradition. A vague benevolence was characteristic of all these ladies, but the only notable efforts to reform society were those of Mrs. Hall, who was interested in prostitutes, street musicians, and "ancient and decayed governesses"; Mrs. Norton, who battled for her children; and the doughty Harriet Martineau, who fought her life long to have her own way. Every one had the storyteller's magic power, all were fluent and persistent and possessed the astonishing vocabulary which almost seems the inheritance of English women.

Their traits were normal: all women wish to be admired, to accomplish something out of the ordinary, to ameliorate suffering, to be powerful. Abnormality consists not in the possession of such traits, but in their overaccentuation. Very often these women wrote because they were unhappy; among them there were two cripples, one was deaf, two had deficient sight; two candid souls admitted intolerable childhoods; not one of them enjoyed good health; Mrs. Craik, who cared most about money, had been very poor. The influences which determined them to become novelists had their beginnings in childhood and lay concealed until they assumed a form and became capable of emergence.

Yet when all is said, they are a gathering of mediocrities. Confrontation with the greatest women novelists of the century would be unfair to these humbler writers. Those four, although they experienced similar compulsions, belonged to the arachnoids, who weave their webs out of their own substance. They presented life, not as the public expected, but as they believed it possible.

The evening comes before the noon

Charlotte Brontë

THE RESOURCES of the Brontë game are inexhaustible. Whenever the players sit back in triumph or in discontent, convinced that no further move is possible, a beneficent hand scatters fresh clues upon the board—the letters to M. Heger, an earthly lover for unearthly Emily, the theories of psychoanalysis, a promise of sport in tracking down each incident in the novels with the object of proving these unhappy girls mere plagiarists, and, latest in time, the liberal hope implicit in the *juvenilia*. Thus the game begins again, to progress under new rules, while, indifferent to its existence, the public flock to Brontë plays and pictures, drawn by the irresistible Brontë spell.

Our present concern is with Charlotte and the relation between her life and her books. It is not our purpose to write a biographical sketch of this passionate, unfortunate woman, the course of her outward career being already familiar; it is to deal with those events and influences which bore directly on her work.

It is perhaps impossible to understand the woman or her novels without a thorough knowledge of her early writings. The peculiar accomplishments of her maturity were the purgation of her childish fantasies and the rebuilding of an amoral world into one which the public of a hundred years has entered with delight. There was nothing unique in this struggle; every novelist must correct his day-dream existence and transfer from his private imagery as much as his readers will be able to accept; but very few write out their wild fancies in extended form, and Charlotte stands alone in the touching completeness of her self-betrayal.

Although we cannot comprehend her creative processes without reading her *juvenilia,* it would be egregious folly to suppose that all the sources of her mature work lie in their closely written lines. The experiences of actual life—housework and study, friendships, travel, love, grief, death—poured their waters into the well of fantasy.

THE PARSONAGE AT HAWORTH was not an unhappy home for little Charlotte. Mrs. Gaskell has made us see it with her own eyes—a bleak, bare place, in contrast with her own Victorian parlor, which was, according to mid-century taste, the prettiest in Manchester. The novelist, meditating biography, crossed to the church to read the memorial tablets and reflect with tears upon Charlotte's mother, who had died young and left many helpless little children to follow her to that sad resting place. She turned to shiver at the outstretched moors and at the graveyard jostling the house wall. When she went home, she described the scene with such poignancy that her readers see the Brontës perpetually in the very act of death. But if we are to understand small Charlotte, we must gently set Mrs. Gaskell aside for a time, while we raise the tombstones and release the brothers and sisters.

The bustle of settling the parsonage had scarcely subsided when Mrs. Brontë entered her last illness. During the seven months remaining to her, the poor woman upstairs in bed worried more about her soul than about her babies. Charlotte had only one memory of her mother; she had seen her bathed in sunlight, playing with little Branwell. She did not know, and was never to learn, what it meant to love a mother nor how mothers feel toward their daughters. Her attempt in *Shirley* to depict the mother and daughter relation of Mrs. Pryor and Caroline was a forlorn failure.

During this first year in Haworth the Brontë family led a confused existence. Not only was the mother isolated upstairs, the six little folk all came down with scarlet fever. Nurses and extra servants crowded the house, and for a time twelve souls lodged under the narrow roof. The father was distracted with anxiety over the wife to whom he was devoted; he suffered the more because, as he expressed it, "the great enemy, envying her life of holiness," scared her with fears of hell. Mr. Brontë had had no time to make friends in his new parish, and, in his helplessness, was forced to go deeply into debt. His wife's sister relieved him of some of his responsibilities when she came from Penzance to nurse Mrs. Brontë. After the funeral, Miss Branwell went back to Penzance to pack up her belongings, and then returned to pass the rest of her life in the parsonage. A dainty, bright-eyed lady, much older than the children's mother, she regretted the pleasures of Penzance and was often very cross. She made the little Brontës feel that she blamed them for the rough weather of Yorkshire and the cold stone floors under her feet.

Aunt Branwell made no pretense of mothering the little Brontës but remained an inflexible maiden aunt. The children's attitude toward her varied from a chill neutrality to positive dislike. Their young hearts were fortified against outsiders; they instinctively formed a Brontë alliance against the world. Papa, harassed, excitable, but affectionate, was within the barrier, but Aunt Branwell was sternly excluded. Mr. Brontë's means were small, but he did his best for his motherless children. He invited the little folk to breakfast with him every morning in his study, and every afternoon he was their guest at tea. Aunt Branwell preferred to eat alone in her room upstairs, but Charlotte and her sisters saw quite enough of her during the tiresome hours spent in the daily sewing lesson, while Papa was teaching Branwell more interesting subjects in the study. In the kitchen, the little girls learned to peel potatoes, make bread, and cook simple dishes. They had brief lessons every day with Papa and were allowed to read all the books in his library. He had written some of them himself: this was a subject for great pride; from the dawn of thought the children conceived an enormous respect for printed matter. Mr. Brontë subscribed to several periodicals and newspapers and, as poor people did and always ought to do, loaned his, and borrowed others from the neighbors. The children were permitted to read everything which came into the house. They owned a few textbooks, and such juveniles as *Robinson Crusoe* and the *Arabian Nights,* but neither they nor their father made any distinction between reading matter suitable for children and that intended for adults.

Meals in the parsonage were plain but well cooked. The house was almost painfully clean, and looked bare to the occasional visitor because it was carpetless and lacked the moreen curtains, hanging like boards at windows and enclosing the beds in funereal gloom, to which people were accustomed in respectable houses. Mr. Brontë could not afford carpeting, and he forbade draperies because he was afraid of fire. Mrs. Brontë had been very nearsighted and the children had inherited the defect; he was terrified lest one of them stumble against the fender. Some uneasiness was rational—Margaret Oliphant carried a scar to her grave from such an accident—

but Mr. Brontë exaggerated his anxiety into a phobia. Charlotte's ambivalent attitude toward fire had its origin in her adoption of her father's fear and in her own longing for warmth and brightness.

Perhaps she grew a little ashamed of the lack of decoration, for when she used the parsonage in her stories, she embellished it with ostentatious ornament. But the outlines of the house were always there; they were indelible. The parsonage was reality itself, the point of departure for imagination, fixed in its place between the moors and the graveyard and St. Michael's. These were symbols in her life story—for the child a house, for the wanderer a moor—for the returned a grave.

Mr. Brontë was confident that he could conduct his son's education, but conceived the necessity of sending the little girls to a school which would fit them to earn their living as governesses. His means gave him small choice of institutions. He decided on Cowan Bridge, which had been recently established and, designed for clergymen's daughters, would assure his girls friends of their own class. He did not enroll all of his daughters at one time, but made a trial with the two older, Maria and Elizabeth. In September, 1824, Charlotte, who was eight, and little Emily, who was only four, joined their sisters, but when the next spring came on, Maria was taken home to die. Elizabeth followed her, first to the parsonage, then to the grave. The bereaved father did not hold the school accountable, and after the midsummer holidays sent Charlotte and Emily back to Cowan Bridge. When they were permanently removed in the autumn of 1825, the reason given was the dampness of the situation, rather than any ill treatment of the little girls.

Cowan Bridge was an abominable institution managed by a stupid, somewhat brutal director. Yet it is unlikely that Charlotte in her brief residence had any personal encounter with Mr. Carus Wilson. She feared the sight of him and detested the school over which he ruled despotically. As she developed, she discovered definite reasons for hating him and persuaded herself that, assisted by a sadistic woman teacher, he had been responsible for her sisters' martyrdom. Mr. Wilson was a symbol of cruelty and strength, qualities which attracted Charlotte as much as they repelled her. This ambivalence established in early childhood was her characteristic attitude toward virile men throughout her life. Mr. Carus Wilson may have been the earliest of the elder brothers, the prototype of the long line of ruthless, brutal characters whom Charlotte, in the disguise of a weak, persistent boy, alternately hated and adored.

She brought other concepts home from Cowan Bridge. A gentle, superior woman teacher would reappear in fiction under the name of Temple, first in *The Spell*, later in *Jane Eyre*. Her opposite, the sadistic, inferior teacher, may have been the original of haughty Zenobia in the early tales, but found an undisputed place in *Jane Eyre*. The sisters, "proud Eliza and proud Georgiana," who figure in the same novels, probably originated in girl visitors to the school whom Charlotte envied and despised. Once, in her adolescence, she was depressed by a dream of her dead sisters, who seemed to have come on a visit—they made fun of the furniture and did not care for the things they had once loved—"proud Eliza" and "proud Georgiana" had disguised themselves as Maria and Elizabeth.

On Charlotte's return to the parsonage, she discovered that the deaths of the older girls had greatly enhanced her importance in the home. She was advanced to be eldest; she had become nine-year-old "Miss Brontë of Haworth." The cult of dead sister worship may have had its inception in the shrewd little girl's feeling that it was wicked to be pleased at her improved estate. Her new situation was conducive to arrogance; in that neighborhood there was no great family with young lady heiresses to outshine the curate's daughter. One reason why Charlotte could ill endure the life of a governess lay in her inability to be reconciled to her social position when she was forced to recognize it.

She did not play the Little Mother role with Emily and Anne; she was the teacher and the Games Mistress. Branwell was younger than Charlotte, but his precocity, his advantage in sex, his courage made him her equal. The brother with whom a Victorian woman novelist grew up usually exerted a stronger influence on her work than the man whom she loved and married. In childhood the relation between Charlotte and Branwell was very close, but he was never the strong, cruel Elder Brother of her fantasy. As the damned soul, Henry Hastings, in "Henry Hastings and His Sister," he was a weakling. Neither in real life nor in her novel did Charlotte permit Branwell to lead her.

The four children enjoyed an immense freedom from supervision. They came promptly to meals, learned lessons, helped with the housework, went to bed at dusk. Their elders, doubtless, believed that they could account for every moment of the young folks' day. In reality they were ignorant of vast tracts of leisure and of cleverly camouflaged enterprise.

The frail Games Mistress organized no rough plays. The children amused themselves quietly except when occasionally they fell to disputing so fiercely that Papa ran out of his study and begged for peace. Sometimes Papa went to Leeds; then he brought home toys, as all good fathers should. When Charlotte was ten, Mr. Brontë returned with a little present for each of his children. No doubt the little girls thanked him dutifully, but it was Branwell's gift of wooden soldiers which everyone coveted. He said each could choose her favorite, although she must understand that he was the real owner of the little men. Charlotte named her choice the Duke of Wellington. In her opinion he was the most commanding, somewhat like Papa, possibly a little like the awful Mr. Carus Wilson. Ever so many new games could be played with the soldiers. The little fellows were renamed as the play of the hour demanded, but each retained surface characteristics and inherent traits by which he could be distinguished.

The children told each other stories about the wooden heroes. It occurred to them that if they wrote down these stories they would be authors—Papa had written books and was an author. Accordingly they began to scribble.

The writing game differed from the rainy day games of other bookish children only in the intensity and unchildish persistence of the players. They toiled at pleasure. Where other youngsters—like the Merivales—acted out their dramas, the Brontës painfully indited theirs. Even in the isolation of the parsonage, they arrived at the idea that they were a peculiar people; that their games were secret and must be kept so; as Charlotte said, in her satisfied way, "All of our plays are very strange ones," an unfortunate conclusion which was probably due to the whispers of admiring servants—unfortunate because it is not good for children to believe themselves set apart.

In these earliest stories she made no definite use of her actual experiences at Cowan Bridge, though "school" was, as with all children, the favorite theme. Her memories were not so fixed nor was the light about them of so lurid a cast as it became after long reflection. Real life seldom provided sufficiently exciting material for the story game, although Charlotte did not disdain its use and one of her neatest compositions was inspired by a fanatic who invaded Tabby's kitchen and declaimed Bible verses, an event which impressed her, not as a religious experience, but as an outlandish occurrence.

But as a rule the children's stories were based on reading rather than on life. The Bible, Shakespeare, and *Pilgrim's Progress* were books found in all cultured homes of the period. Walter Scott's influence on the Brontës, as on every budding romancist, was immeasurably potent. But they had also access to Byron's poetry, which was not generally considered fit reading for young girls; and they read newspapers which printed, besides political information, reports of sordid crimes and executions. The fantasies of the *Arabian Nights* and James Hogg's tales of apparitions were eagerly devoured by these little cormorants.

The imaginary country of which Charlotte and her brother were overlords was Angria, perhaps derived from Anglia, although it lay in Africa. A geography with fascinating pictures gave an impetus to the play, and in the earliest days it was thrilling to imagine the wooden men crossing rough seas and scaling vast mountains. Not much invention, but industry and a strong pictorial sense were necessary in order to play the writing game properly. The names of places and characters were usually taken from books, but when they originated in the neighborhood, they could be made to sound outlandish by a change in spelling or pronunciation. Many African regions were formed from pictures in the geography, but there were moors in Angria like those about Haworth, and the Angrian cathedral of St. Michael's was an enlargement of little St. Michael's church where father preached. When a palace was required, the parsonage was improved, picked up, and set down in the suburbs of Verdopolis, the capital, without the slightest jar.

Paper on which to write the stories was precious. It has been suggested that the tiny books, similar in size to a modern packet of cigarette matches, were made to scale with the wooden soldiers, but it is likely that the children did not think of these characters as little, even while actually handling them. Nor was economy the only motive for the microscopic writing; the intensity of the Brontë concentration and the "secret" nature of the game induced them to fit their stories into the smallest possible space. Papa Brontë, sympathizing with the ardent young authors, occasionally contributed a notebook with an edict to the effect that what the children wrote within its covers must be legible. Charlotte's writing was much neater than Branwell's, but she was older. There is often a likable scribble toward the last of Branwell's lines as if he, for one, felt he had worked quite long enough.

The shocking case of the resurrectionists, who murdered with the object of filling a doctor's standing order for bodies, was a motif with many Victorian writers whose youth had been frightened by the Burke and Hare case, but fourteen-year-old Charlotte Brontë was probably the youngest to make literary use of it. The idea of disinterring the newly dead was peculiarly horrible to a little girl who lived hard by a churchyard, and with some ingenuity she discovered a way to mitigate its terrors: suppose one opened the grave and found in the coffin—not a horrid corpse, but something precious. So Charlotte wrote a story in which the Chief Librarian buried a coffin at midnight. The following night, body snatchers disinterred it but, to their confusion and rage, found it contained only books stolen from the Public Library.

The child's endeavor to escape from her morbid thoughts of death is pathetic, but the effort itself showed an astonishing lack of schooling. The tiny writing deteriorated as the hand tired, she left the *h* out of whisper, as no doubt she did in speech, wrote *coincide* when she meant *collide,* slipped in grammar—"one of the graves were open"— and said the villain "slinked" away.

Charlotte, living hard by the church and graveyard, knew death's ugliest aspects—the black, unflowered coffin and the shower of gravel as it rattled from her father's hand into the open grave. When in the long-lived Brontë game, Branwell, boy fashion, insisted on wars and heaps of slain, Charlotte used her magical powers to resuscitate the dead, not entirely because the fun could not go on without them but because bringing the dead to life was a fine way to rob the grave of its terror.

As little girls, Victorian women novelists read very much the same books: George Eliot possessed in addition a joke book; Eliza Lynn Linton pored over Fox's *Book of Martyrs.* Charlotte's access to newspapers and magazines was somewhat exceptional, although Margaret Oliphant may be said to have been brought up on *Blackwood's Edinburgh Magazine.* But Margaret's early writings gave very little indication of personal sources, and it is Charlotte whose literary history presents a unique opportunity to trace motifs taken over from a magazine story and emerging at intervals from the unconscious.

In August, 1827, when Charlotte was in her impressionable twelfth year, *Blackwood's Magazine* published a tale by James Hogg on the theme of a paternal apparition seen by two brothers. Both these young men love Ellen, a farmer's daughter. The younger is a student, eager to marry her. The elder, the laird's heir, wishes to make her his mistress. The younger brother discovers the elder in an amorous scuffle with the girl, in which, encouraged by a cackling old aunt, he urges her toward the bed. In the subsequent quarrel between the young men, the good brother is made to appear the offender, ostensibly because the other is superior in years and station but, more insidiously, because he is gay and lawless. The heir bids Ellen choose between respectability with his brother and shame with him. Ellen promptly decides to be mistress rather than wife. Not content with victory, the heir challenges his brother to a duel in order to punish his insolence. The apparition of the father, who in the body is two hundred miles away, prevents the duel. He orders his heir to marry Ellen. The elder brother obeys and twelve children are born of the union.

Charlotte felt that the weakness of the student was contemptible, but in her own frailty associated herself with him: the strength, brutality, and success of the elder brother filled her with mingled yearning and aversion. The conqueror was a little like the Duke of Wellington, a little perhaps like the awful Wilson of Cowan Bridge.

The theme of the two brothers was destined to wind its tortuous way through much of her mature writing. Even in *Jane Eyre,* where it does not rise above the surface, Rochester attributes some responsibility for his calamitous marriage to the machinations of his elder brother, Rowland. In the tales and novelettes of the *juvenilia* the brothers are aristocrats; in Charlotte's first mature novel, *The Professor,* they appear in plebian form; in *Shirley,* they are exotics, transplantations from the Continent; in the late fragment "Ellin Hall" recurs the motif of the *juvenilia,* the unresolved struggle between the tyrannical elder brother and his suffering victim—Charlotte herself.

Occasional phrases buried themselves in the little girl's memory to rise again, probably without her recognition of their source. "Two hundred miles away" echoes in "The Spell," in *Shirley,* in the fragment she sent Coleridge. Louis's abrupt announcement in *Shirley* that he will have twelve children sounds like a meaningless resurgence. Ellen Nussey was Charlotte's best friend and Ellen one of the commonest of names, but Ellin in "Ellin Hall," Ellin in the fragment "Emma," both of which retain the stamp of childhood, suggest a hark back to the old grim tale.

The innocent little girl, fascinated by the charms of an amoral world, created one of her own. She had some childish faults; perhaps along with comparatively little instruction in spelling, Cowan Bridge had taught her the fun of spying and concealment's joy. Her early stories depended upon information brought to Lord Charles (Charlotte) by servants whom that young rascal hired to report the unsavory doings of their betters. Lord Charles was ten years old; his motive was the avenging of real or fancied slights. The other characters united in disliking Lord Charles (Charlotte), so that conflict was always in progress—Charlotte against society.

Curiosity is the prime requisite of the novelist. Charlotte's development furnishes a beautiful example of greedy inquisitiveness transformed into the fiction writer's proper interest in character, motive, and action. The value of the *juvenilia* lies not in the crude productions themselves, but in the vision they permit of the gradual molding of spirit and of the form which spirit fashions; coarse speech, brutal deeds, perplexities as to sexual passion which disturbed the mind of the little girl either disappeared as the inner life developed, or were so wrought upon as to become shapes fit to delight the readers of the century.

Mr. Brontë could foresee no better future for his daughter than that of a governess. Although a university man, he was intellectually much inferior to Mrs. Gaskell's father, the Unitarian minister, who, when his daughter's boarding-school days were over, was able to fit her for a superior teaching position. Charlotte, untaught at home, must go to school and make the most of what she could pick up there.

She was nearing fifteen when her father sent her to Roe Head. This was her first opportunity to live a normal life. Who has not pictured her arrival, the very scared, very small young person, determined to do her duty although grimly expectant of rebuffs and mountainous difficulties? The Misses Wooler kept the smallest of boarding schools; there were never more than ten students during the year and a half of Charlotte's residence. Both teachers and pupils learned to like the odd little girl very much; among them she made three lifelong friends, the excellent Miss Wooler, Ellen Nussey, and Mary Taylor. Although she was nearsighted and had not the strength to play games, story-telling made her popular. The wild tales she had heard from ignorant Tabby and incautious Papa, or read for herself in *Blackwood's* and in the newspapers, provided as much excitement as the other girls could endure. Her personal confidences came in rare bursts: once she boasted of the home magazine, told a story from it, and actually promised to show her friends the manuscript. She could not, however, persuade herself to produce this tangible evidence of the dream world.

Probably no one at Haworth had mentioned Charlotte's big nose and irregular mouth—certainly Branwell and the little sisters had not noticed it—and at Roe Head gentle Ellen Nussey never considered that Charlotte was very plain. But brusque Mary Taylor announced the fact, which Charlotte did not venture to dispute. She had pretty enough hair and passable green eyes, but her teeth were poor and, in a period when large, "fine women" were admired, she was unfortunate in being very small. However, her ingenuity had already found ways in which even the fear of death could be mitigated, and, although, like George Eliot, she never ceased to resent her lack of beauty and to embarrass people by talking about it, she was able to turn her defects to advantage in the dream world. The concept of the ugly woman who is more seductive than the beauty dawned early upon Charlotte; it may not be a wholly satisfying vision, but it has a compensating charm.

Although Miss Wooler was not qualified to teach style and composition to a young author, she could set a splendid example as a story-teller. Nature had given her a dramatic delivery and her memory was stored with exciting incidents. The girls loved their schoolmistress and made it a matter of rivalry who should walk nearest her as she paced the long parlor of an evening telling tales of the riots in the hard years before and after Waterloo. The house at Roe Head was comfortable and large. There were bookcases at the end of the parlor and in the center stood a long table draped in a crimson cloth. Cold little Charlotte warmed herself at the fire and in the cheerful color. She admired Miss Wooler's custom of pacing the floor and brought it home to the parsonage. In her stories she painted the walls with rose, and, when she could afford to alter the rooms at Haworth, she brightened them with crimson draperies.

Charlotte had refused meat since she had seen the doctor spit out the horrid mess served at Cowan Bridge. Probably her teeth already hurt her—it was not long before there were many gaps among them —and it was difficult to chew tough mutton. The girls at Roe Head coaxed her with gravy and by degrees persuaded her to eat more as they did. But her poor little nervous stomach gave her bad dreams. In the night, Maria and Elizabeth, the maiden martyrs, of whom she was so proud that she had told her friends how good and clever they had been, seemed to be down in the parlor; they were dressed as grandly as the "proud Eliza" and "the proud Georgiana"; they poked fun at the furniture and cared no longer for the days and joys of old. We do not know how early Charlotte began to dream of carrying the wailing baby along the aisle of Haworth church. In the superstitious fancies to which she was even more given than most of her generation, she supposed this dream presaged misfortune. She used it in *Jane Eyre* because she felt a literary need of it, but perhaps she hoped also that confession would free her from its malign power.

She was as happy at Roe Head as it was possible for her to be anywhere, but the period of her schooling was brief. In July, 1832, she returned to Haworth to serve an apprenticeship by teaching Emily and Anne. She had been a matter of months at Cowan Bridge and only a year and a half at Roe Head; she had had no other formal education when she went out as a governess. It was probably her youth which saved both her and some unfortunate family from her taking a situation immediately, but the prolongation of the home interval was due to the Brontë inertia. Later Charlotte freed herself from this inability to act, but her present wish was very strongly in favor of staying where she was. To Ellen she wrote sedately that life was running a "delightful, though somewhat monotonous course" and furnished her with a day's timetable in which the hours were nicely apportioned between reading, sewing, walking, dining, teaching, and drawing.

In reality Charlotte's life was very far from monotony; she was swept along upon a turbulent stream of imagination and, as she pictured the same scene repeatedly to herself, was continually enchanted by some novel aspect. While Charlotte and Branwell lived and wrote in Angria, Emily and her small satellite were scribbling Gondal chronicles. All four saw their characters in more definite outlines than the flesh and blood folk of Haworth. They attempted with passion to transfer these images to paper, drawing with such prodigious industry that poor Papa Brontë, misled by their fervor, supposed it an indication of talent, and engaged a drawing master from Leeds at the crippling expense of two guineas the visit.

Charlotte's heroines were modeled on the swan-necked ladies in *Friendship's Offering* and *The Keepsake,* exquisite books laid out upon the parlor tables of the genteel—even the parsonage boasted a recent volume. Under the pseudonym of Lord Charles, she wrote a Who's Who of the Angrian court and called it "A Peep into a Picture Book." While the appearance of her chosen characters was derived from published engravings, she continued to use the landscape and architecture of Yorkshire. With Branwell she had the rare treat of a visit to "The Rydings," the estate of Ellen's brother. The rookery, the turret, the well-planned grounds struck audible admiration from the boy, while Charlotte in demure silence seized the house for Angria.

Her invention was weak, but her imagination terrifying in its intensity. When she needed a secluded villa in which her hero Zamorna could install a favorite mistress, Charlotte had only to appropriate the name Cross of Rivaux from a ruined Yorkshire abbey, and in that retired situation set up Haworth parsonage with the improvements she had noted on her brief excursions. While at home only the hardiest plants would thrive, at the Cross of Rivaux roses bloomed over a trellised porch. At home, Aunt's pattens clattered up the cold stone stair; but in Mina Laury's villa, a "brilliant" carpet covered the halls and steps. There the dove-colored walls of the parsonage parlor blushed to "a fine, pale red"; Papa Brontë forbade curtains, but Mina Laury's hangings were "artistical draperies of dark blue silk covered with gold waves and flowers." Charlotte's descriptions show not only her intense pleasure in ornament and color but her longing to be like other people and to possess the very things she pretended to despise.

As yet Charlotte's male characters retained much of the inhuman quality of the little wooden men. The Iron Duke ceased to be her hero and was replaced by his son, the Marquis of Douro, usually called Zamorna, a gloomy, ruthless, satirical, unprincipled, darkly handsome paragon who, when in the mood, could show himself marvelously tender. The ladies adored Zamorna, that masochist's delight; and from their ranks he selected a succession of wives and mistresses. Charlotte had made him up of odd parts, not all of which were original with her. The tyrant hero of eighteenth-century fiction dominated her imagination; if she read Mrs. Inchbald's *A Simple Story*, she must have felt the charm of Dorriforth increase with his "implacability"; for herself she desired a cruel master. Zamorna could be as terrifying as Mr. Carus Wilson or Papa in a temper, but he was sometimes as gay and whimsical as Hogg's Elder Brother.

Zamorna's little brother, the imp Lord Charles, who was Charlotte in disguise, employed his considerable talents in ferreting out the motives and acts of the demonic hero. Ostensibly he hated Zamorna, but in reality he suffered from the conflict between this open enmity and a secret, passionate love for its object. Charlotte (Lord Charles) felt she ought to abominate Zamorna, but could not free herself from his fascination.

Branwell insisted on introducing war and politics into the tales. Charlotte's own interest in such subjects was tepid, but their introduction served to cover her absorption in the struggles of love and jealousy. At the close of Charlotte's literary career, Mrs. Oliphant observed correctly that her only theme had been the battle of the sexes. Had Mrs. Oliphant seen the *juvenilia,* and had her consternation at the contents permitted her to finish reading, she would have been amazed at the manner in which Charlotte refined and muted the eroticism of her adolescence.

Such an achievement lay far in the young writer's future. Throughout her teens and early twenties she was wrapt in fantasy and appeared incapable of literary or ethical progress. Her vocabulary was not better than that of other girls of bookish tastes. She possessed a poetic fluency, but it was not more remarkable than was general among young British writers. In self-criticism she was wholly lacking, largely because the audience of home demanded nothing beyond excitement, and as yet she had worked for no other public. Her chief assets were her superb power of feeling and seeing the inner drama, and her unresting persistence in attempting to project her fantasy in words.

The tone of these early stories was antisocial. Little Lord Charles, the author, wrote in order to revenge himself on Zamorna. In "Albion and Marina," alternative names for Zamorna and his first wife, he went the length of representing Marina as dead in order to punish his abhorred brother. Charlotte was eighteen when she wrote *The Spell,* but the motif had not altered; as Lord Charles she wished vengeance on her elder brother and proposed to furnish circumstantial evidence of his insanity. *The Spell* is an unsatisfactory study of the *Doppelgänger,* which leaves the reader with all the questions on his own hands: he must settle for himself the number and identity of the brothers; his the speculation whether or not Zamorna, "the young man of promise," will die in a madhouse. For us the chief interest lies in the malign Lord Charles and his fierce desire for vengeance. This thirst Charlotte was never to exorcize.

As a mature writer she corrected faults of a meaner order, such as spying and plagiarism. In her early prose, she took whatever she wanted from available sources. The preface to *The Spell* sounds as if inspired by one of Shakespeare's bastards, Zamorna's madness hints at Hamlet, the building of the city rises from the infernal kingdom of *Paradise Lost,* the dwarf Fidic is compounded of Scott's Goblin Page and Fenella. The chronic sunlessness of nature, the coffin-filled niches of the dim, vast cathedral, the avenues of "tall dark trees leading to a church yard" reflect the Gothic romances of the period. However, after she began to write with a view to publication she was exceedingly careful to avoid plagiarism, and if the weird Ulrica influenced the fate of Mrs. Rochester, it must be said for Charlotte that the Saxon hag and the burning battlements had become the common property of Victorian novelists, who produced them as artlessly as if they were slices of bread and butter from a communal pantry.

In her early writings, Charlotte's little fingers snatched, not only at characters in books, but at people and incidents in the actual world, which she dragged into her fantasy with touching naïveté. For example, when Zamorna first meets the daughter of haughty Northumberland for whose sake he will set aside his first wife—as Napoleon had not so long since repudiated Josephine—he pulls a music stool to her side at the tea table—it is his favorite seat—a wonderfully informal position for the demonic hero to occupy; a parsonage custom must have found its way into Angrian court circles.

But the realism with which Charlotte bleakly describes the diminished funeral cortege of Zamorna's heir is impressive. Here the author who lived next the graveyard speaks with authority of "a coach with the corpse, the undertaker's barouche," and a single carriage. Along with these childish plagiarisms and transferences from personal experience were wisps of occurrences in the outer world which Charlotte, birdlike, wove into her nest. Newspapers and magazines had filled columns with the amazing career of Edward Irving, deposed minister of the Church of Scotland, whose death occurred in 1834. In 1836 Charlotte described Zamorna's second wife as entering the house, where he has installed his mistress, under the assumed name of Mrs. Irving, wife of the minister of a northern kirk.

Charlotte's early writings were exceedingly coarse. A blustering young aristocrat refers to a dead baby as taking "a ride in the cold meat cart." Slang and bad grammar, drunkenness and wantonness abound; oaths are bandied, brutal kicks and blows bestowed. Zamorna rifles a lady's desk and reads her private letters with a sneer—an action which Louis Moore repeats in *Shirley* in a less offensive manner. A general purgation was necessary before her work was fit reading for a mid-century public. To accuse Papa Brontë of being the source of unsavory knowledge seems ridiculous in view of the nature of his correspondence and the testimony of his friends; Branwell was too young to pay any but the most infrequent stolen visits to the Black Bull; Charlotte's ideas and language were largely derived from reading.

She was amazingly naïve. At twenty she described Zamorna sitting in his mistress's boudoir for three hours while he writes letters; during this arduous occupation he wears his copper helmet with "impending plumes." At last Mina Laury timidly ventures to remove the casque, to rearrange the ringlets on his "fevered brow" and caress his "luxuriant whiskers." He submits graciously to this mollifying treatment but, when Mina Laury ventures to plead for permission to accompany him to the front, he informs her sternly that it was not Alexander but Darius who "carried his concubines to the war."

Zamorna's mistress, Miss Laury, is one of the more respectable characters in Angria, a good-hearted wench, who likes children and knows her place: "Female acquaintance she never sought, nor if she had sought would she have found them." A rehearsal for the garden scene in *Jane Eyre* occurs between Mina Laury and Zamorna: in the spirit of cruel teasing with which Rochester was to threaten Jane with Bitternut Lodge, Zamorna tells Mina of his wish to bestow her on an inferior noble.

Lady Zenobia's passion for Zamorna drives her to madness. This tall beauty is reputed to have had a wrestling match with her husband; the struggle between Rochester and his insane wife is a curious refinement on the theme. Charlotte seems to have admired and feared Zenobia, who may have had an original in the world of reality as the teacher who maltreated Maria at Cowan Bridge. The quality of strength, however ill used, fascinated the frail Charlotte.

Earliest of the conceptions of Angrian ladies is Marian Hume, Zamorna's first wife, a gentle, delicate girl derived from the conventional heroine in novels of the early nineteenth century. With tender ferocity Zamorna persuades her to give place to his new love Mary Percy. She consents and dies, heartbroken, when her child is born.

Her successor, Mary Percy, is a girl of spirit whose jealousy of her husband's mistress is accounted to her as sin in Angrian circles, because she thus sets herself in opposition to Zamorna. Fidic, the dwarf, expresses the current moral view when he says reproachfully, "So long as Zamorna's love was yours, what mattered it if it was not wholly yours?"

Charlotte's own relation to her hero was painful and complex. Her conscience told her Zamorna was evil, and yet she admired and loved him. It was in vain that she disguised herself as horrid little Lord Charles whose sole ambition was to plague and punish Zamorna. Behind the mask of fury hid poor Charlotte, a creature panting for love or, if love might not be, for abuse. There is one sorry scene in which Zamorna bends kindly enough, over a group of children; Lord Charles cannot resist kissing the dark face. But Zamorna wipes off the caress and gives the boy a scornful push. Charlotte was twenty-one and had had a proposal of marriage when she wrote obscurely of Zamorna, "People say I am not in earnest when I abuse him." Of all the Angrians she and her brother were the only ones who understood the morality of the real world; the others were governed by such motives as the wish to please Zamorna, ambition, and love of intrigue. Charlotte, although her nature was secretive, longed to confess and to be justified. When in solemn hours the power of fantasy weakened, she was distressed by a sense of guilt. She did not know how to bridge the chasm between her turbulent inner life and her modest existence in the actual world. Nor did she desire to do so, because the "infernal world" was very much to her liking.

The motif frequently spoken of as the Call, which would some day fascinate readers of *Jane Eyre,* had been used in "Albion and Marina" and was repeated in *The Spell;* the execrable scene in which Zamorna and his double presented themselves before the Royal Family was refined to a charming whimsicality when in *Shirley* the Moores bid their cousin Caroline decide who is Robert and who is

Louis. The characters of Miss Temple and the proud sisters in *The Spell* was enormously improved upon in *Jane Eyre*, although they retained their original quality.

The most dramatic scene in *The Spell* was destined to be played out in real life. Zamorna springs from the bed on which he lies dying, and, armed with a brace of pistols, exclaims, "I shall no longer lie waiting the issue like a helpless child, but rise and meet death as a man should do, face to face!" Alas for Branwell! Did this wretched rodomontade lodge within the recesses of his ruined mind until the day came when he too dreamt that he must rise and greet the conqueror death?

When Charlotte chronicled the ravings of Zamorna, Branwell was a boy of seventeen, hope of the Brontës, and as yet no drunkard and innocent of drugs. Yet Zamorna's shrieks to his "white witch," his "seraphic hypocrite," whom he suspects of poisoning him, prefigure those excesses of *Wuthering Heights* and *The Tenant of Wildfell Hall* which Branwell has been credited with inspiring. Thus Branwell, far from leading the way, followed the downward course which he and his sisters plotted for their demonic heroes. The Rake's Progress, in which all but Anne exulted, became his destiny. Charlotte's theory that Zamorna, "the young man of promise," would die in a madhouse prefigured Branwell's shocking fate. But she predicted this four years before her brother began to drink.

A year after the completion of *The Spell*, Charlotte returned to Miss Wooler's school as a teacher, with Emily in tow in the role of pupil. The younger girl already knew all her sister could teach her except for a knowledge of reading French, nor is it probable that anyone at Roe Head had more than Charlotte to offer a pupil. Emily, who would be able to endure Brussels because there she could learn something, was bored and unhappy at Miss Wooler's. She fell ill and returned to Haworth, yielding her place to docile Anne, the only one of the young Brontës who was a citizen of the real world. Ellen Nussey lived near by. The older girls exchanged letters and saw each other often, but Ellen and Anne had temporarily more in common than Ellen and Charlotte because both were intensely religious. The Evangelical movement was at its height; everywhere people examined their inner lives and attempted to make their "hearts right with God." Papa Brontë was an Evangelical who had formerly been a Presbyterian; the girls' mother had been a Methodist; it was natural for Anne to yield to the most potent influence of the times; it would have been natural for Charlotte, had not ambivalent memories of the hateful parson of Cowan Bridge rankled, had it not been for the barriers of Angria. To be wholly Ellen's and God's meant the surrender of the "infernal world" and the tearing of Zamorna from her heart. As she read the Bible, sometimes her load lightened, but no wellspring of grace sprang up within her thirsting soul. A longing to confess racked her. She wrote to Ellen, "If you knew my thoughts; the dreams that absorb me; and the fiery imagination that at times eats me up"; but here her secretive nature warned her against further self-betrayal; and she added an hypocritical protest against the insipidity of society "as it is." She knew nothing of this world's society, but yearned for the excitement of Zamorna's court.

She hated the teaching which filled her days; she hated the evenings when she had to sit with the pupils in Miss Wooler's parlor and dared not write of the Angrians lest the others wonder at her intense emotion. "Except in total solitude, I scarce dare think of them," she wrote, and the only solitude was in her curtained bed, where dreams possessed the waking girl. When morning came, the chains which bound her to "the world below" were lengthened, but not struck off: "All this day I have been in a dream, half-miserable, half-ecstatic,—miserable because I could not follow it out uninterruptedly, ecstatic because it showed almost in the vivid light of reality the ongoings of the infernal world."

Naturally she detested the pupils who interrupted such reveries, although the unfortunate girls had no intention of annoying Miss Wooler's favorite. Yet Charlotte found them unforgivable and in private called them "dolts, fat-headed oafs, and asses."

Miss Wooler moved her school to Dewsbury Moor, where Anne caught a severe cold. Charlotte, remembering the unwholesome location of Cowan Bridge and the deaths of the little maiden martyrs, Elizabeth and Maria, decided that the situation on Dewsbury Moor was unhealthful. She raged at Miss Wooler as if the good soul had been plotting against Anne, until the lady wept copiously. The sick girl was sent home, but Charlotte, who worried not only about her younger sister but about Emily slaving in an Exeter school, grew more lonely, more unhappy, more hopeless of matching the infernal world with anything worth half so much as her dreams, until she too fell ill and returned to Haworth. Ellen's brother, a young parson who needed a wife to help him in his school, asked her to marry him, but the girl who could not give up Angria for Ellen and God could scarcely resign her magic land in response to a business proposition. In the summer of 1839 a second and very silly suitor suggested matrimony after one evening's acquaintance. Charlotte brushed this aside.

Between these unflattering offers, she passed three months as a governess in a private family. She was twenty-three, quite old enough to earn her own living. But she was very difficult, very nervous, disliked children, and had an exaggerated respect for the social claims of Miss Brontë of Haworth. The practical Sidgwicks supposed she was their children's rather incompetent governess who was an excellent seamstress.

When she returned to Haworth, she conceived the idea of writing for publication in order to escape from her drudging life. She had not lost her belief in Branwell's genius, and the two maintained a loose literary partnership. He wrote desperate letters to Wordsworth and Blackwood; Charlotte consulted kind-hearted Southey, and sent a specimen of her work to Hartley Coleridge, an excerpt which showed an attempt to introduce characters and scenes of the "infernal world" into the actual life of Yorkshire. Coleridge was not favorably impressed, and Charlotte, pained at his criticism, wrote him a pert letter which she signed C.T. for Charles Townshend, one of the names of Zamorna's brother.

Two long stories completed the *juvenilia*. "Caroline Vernon" bears no date but is obviously less mature than "Henry Hudson and His Sister." The published version has been improved in a literary sense by rearrangement, but such editing is especially undesirable as the story merits reading merely because of the light it throws on Charlotte's development.

Caroline is a girl of fifteen, passionately in love with Zamorna, husband of her half-sister and already the father of a family. She passes a year in the capital without seeing him, but at its conclusion decides that since his "neglect augmented passion" she will again put herself in his way. Zamorna welcomes the opportunity. In a spirited scene, he declares, "If I were a beardless Turk, Caroline, I would take you to my harem"; but, either because eastern luxury is out of Angrian bounds, or because he cherishes his whiskers, he contents himself with carrying her to a house on the verge of a moor near a little church. It is impossible to ignore Charlotte's association with her impulsive heroine, and, although there is something pathetic in her naïveté, it is equally impossible not to be amused at Charlotte ruthlessly exiling Papa, Branwell, Emily, Anne, and Tabby in order to accommodate Zamorna and herself in Haworth parsonage. In "Caroline Vernon" she preserved two versions of her favorite theme, seduction in a garden. Here, as earlier in *The Spell* and as later in *Jane Eyre,* the hero irritates his victim's nerves by an assumption of mocking indifference and, when he has broken her resistance, shows himself tender and passionate.

The last of Charlotte's *juvenilia,* "Henry Hudson and His Sister," was finished March 20, 1839, within a month of her twenty-third birthday. She was almost four years older than was Margaret Oliphant when the latter wrote her first published novel. Charlotte's last juvenile production was a wretched piece of work, but it was of a higher moral order than its predecessors, being motivated by the self-denying love of a girl for her brother. The characters were more firmly defined, Zamorna had yielded the position of hero to Sir William Percy, and the action took place in England. Thus the story built a frail bridge between Charlotte's private world and that which a public, not overly nice, might be willing to accept. Coarse language, bad grammar, profanity and clichés, bathos, the foppish but brutal nature of the hero, the dimness of scenes which were so actual to the writer that she saw no need for sharper portrayal, impaired the tale, which would be better lost did it not show the romancist in the latest stage of emergence from her subjective world.

The heroine is Charlotte's double, a plain, small, clever girl employed as a companion-governess. Her soul, "Smothered under diffidence and prudence and a skilful address," threatens at times to "burst forth like lava." Her old father dwells far away among "dreary moors." She knows that her brother is a rogue, but neither the murder he has committed nor the shameful punishment of his crime has weakened her love: as she expresses it, "Natural affection is a thing never rooted out where it has really existed."

This "pale and pinched" governess loves and is dishonorably loved by Sir William Percy. Fearing the vengeance of her father and brother, she refuses to be his mistress. The favorite garden scene takes place in a graveyard beside a marble tomb, beneath a giant yew. One word gleams on that nameless tomb—*Resurgam*—for beneath it lies one of the many lost ladies whom the profligate Zamorna has betrayed. Here Elizabeth encounters Sir William and repulses him, slipping "from his hold like an apparition," scurrying back three miles to town, her virtue intact. Had a seducer crossed Charlotte's path, she would have known as well as any woman in England how to deal with him.

Charlotte's entire experience as governess in private houses amounted to only one year. In March, 1841, when she was almost twenty-five, she entered a family by the name of White, who took a genuine interest in her. Mr. White offered her the only kind of advice she was capable of accepting—that which chimed in with her own desires. She was longing to travel. Her school friend, Mary Taylor, had been writing letters from the Continent which made Charlotte frantic with yearning to escape from her duties. Mr. White suggested that the only way she could get on in the world was to have a school of her own and, to make that a success, she must be able to offer special attractions such as competent instruction in French.

Charlotte's half-hearted attempt to interest Hartley Coleridge was probably a first effort at shaping her outer life. This second endeavor met with success. She wrote a coaxing letter to Aunt Branwell, and after making sure of funds from that not ungenerous source, decided to take Emily and settle Anne in Haworth with the old people. All that she did was just and sensible, and yet Charlotte seems to have brought on the Brontë fates. Hitherto her work had been purely subjective and had not emerged from story into reality. Her conscious will was at variance with the deep forces which impelled her, and she worked mischief where she intended good.

From the first she felt a strong wish to go to Brussels rather than to Lille. Her anxious letter to Madame Heger, mistress of a girls' school in the Belgian capital, brought a kindly answer. The Hegers were comparatively young people with small children. Charlotte's letter had touched them, and they named a flat rate in order not to confuse their English correspondent with an itemized list of probable expenses.

If the Hegers marveled at the advanced age of the new pupils and at their odd costumes, their politeness enabled them to conceal it. M. Heger thought Emily had the better mind and noticed that she imposed on Charlotte, who seemed neither to resent nor perhaps to perceive that her sister presumed on her good-nature. Yet Charlotte took violent dislikes to the personnel and the pupils. Her schoolmates were "animals," but the names she called them were not worse than those she had applied to Miss Wooler's poor girls.

Emily opposed an imperturbable front to the great city, but Charlotte grudgingly yielded to its influence. New faces, scenes, customs, foods were studied and memorized if not approved. M. Heger was a gifted teacher with a feeling for form and a dislike of extravagance.

He deserved credit for much of the immense advance of *The Professor* over "Henry Hastings and His Sister."

Form may be molded from without but is essentially the expression of the soul. Charlotte owed much to Heger the teacher, but infinitely more to Heger the man. Without any consciousness on his part, he displaced the image of the profligate Zamorna and the cold fop Sir William Percy. The moral benefit of love for a human being, for an honorable man of a well-defined character, a man of intelligence and charm, was of inestimable value to the woman and, working through her, to her books. M. Heger did not return the love of the plain, withering English spinster; his own wife suited him. But those sentimentalists who regret that Charlotte's love met no response will do well to remember how much better it was for her to love Heger than to waste herself on Zamorna.

Aunt Branwell's death, which summoned the sisters to Haworth, was found not to be an unmixed evil. The little treasures which the girls inherited seemed less wonderful than in the old days when they had admired them, as they rested their eyes from the fine seam. But the money she left gave her nieces a feeling of confidence in the future when, on their father's death, they would have to vacate the old house. The fourth part of Miss Branwell's £1500 to each was a fortune to girls who had nothing.

Charlotte could afford to return to Brussels and was wildly anxious to do so, although Emily stubbornly refused to accompany her. There seems to have been no thought of substituting submissive Anne, and it is likely that in her heart Charlotte did not desire either sister as a companion.

Since she was now attached to the staff as a part-time teacher,

Madame Heger had an excellent excuse for inviting her with less frequency to the family sitting room; the other teachers might take offense if Miss Brontë were singled out for special favors. Madame had little reason to like Charlotte: she was a devout Catholic, and the English girl abhorred the Roman Church; she was a Belgian, and Charlotte sneered at Belgian culture. She was vexed also at signs of the foreigner's infatuation for her husband and dreaded the unpredictable behavior of this peculiar girl; a scandal would ruin them all.

Charlotte now occupied a position comparable to that of George Eliot in the houses of Dr. Brabant and John Chapman: she was the single woman pitted against the wife. Wounded by the deepening chill in Madame Heger's manner, desperately anxious to justify herself, scared but determined not to be driven from the field, she grew ever more nervous, more unhappy, nearer despair. There were times when she sought refuge from the torment of the real world in the fantasy which had so nearly lost its hold. As she lay sleepless in one of the white curtained beds scattered along the vast length of the dormitory, like tents upon the desert, and she herself a wanderer, encamped without hope, she reverted "fanatically as ever to the old ideas, the old faces, and the old scenes in the world below." It seems unlikely that she returned alone to that sunless land; for her powers were those of the mermaid, whose love has lighted on a mortal, who clasps him, drags him down through the waters to the caverns of the sea king.

At length the real world ruled by Madame Heger became too strong for her. The position was hopeless, and she went despairing home to Haworth, leaving, perhaps, a gift for the unresponsive M. Heger, an exquisitely bound book of her stories in manuscript; after she became famous, he or another added the author's name.

She had little to give, and this might serve to remind him of her without giving offense to his wife. But she did not go with a heart full of charity toward that lady; little Louise Heger heard, or thought she heard, the English lady murmur to her mother, "Je me vengerai."

She went home to misery. The letters she wrote M. Heger, although their contents had been strangely anticipated in the correspondence of Angria, have a pathos in which the earlier effusions are wanting. But they are not entirely honest, because she wished the obdurate Heger to pity, if he would not love. Thus she took over her father's incipient blindness, and complained that she could not write her stories as she used, lest they cost her sight. Beneath the surface lay truth; she could not write because she had been driven out of Angria by her love for a human; in the world of here and now she waited, homeless and shivering, for new sight, new subjects, new ways of creation.

The Brontë sisters prepared to keep a school as if they were playing a dreary game in which not one of them believed. Letters were written, a prospectus issued; they admitted with relief that Haworth was too isolated to attract pupils. Besides, Papa Brontë's eyes were in a sad condition and Branwell was behaving badly; they were pleased to find themselves abandoning a scheme which had perhaps been attempted merely because Aunt Branwell had lent money on that understanding; not one of the girls would have been able to misappropriate a penny.

Yet honest Charlotte's word was not to be trusted when the subject involved her emotions. What she wished to believe was true for her, and she would have suffered martyrdom rather than give up an idea she had seized. Something of the value of the romancist lies in this power to cling to a personal belief. Charlotte's house-party scenes are frequently condemned because people do not behave as she saw Mr. Rochester's guests behaving; but it is not the mission of such romancists to show us how the Ingrams and their friends look in the eyes of the general public; what Charlotte had to do was to pass on her impressions. Many a shy, sensitive woman has found them valid. But much which we can explain in the author vexes us in the woman. Charlotte was not sincere when she justified the sisters' chosen pseudonyms as due to "conscientious scruples at assuming Christian names positively masculine." Anne was capable of such scruples, but we can not credit Emily with them, nor Charlotte, who had from earliest youth signed herself Lord Charles, Captain Tree, Charles Townshend.

The first mature novel, *The Professor* (1857), which was not published during her lifetime, is the only one which shows directly the restraining hand of M. Heger. His methods had been drastic and her own mood was coldly quiet after the subsidence of tumultuous passion. It is an admirably constructed novel, but its restraint and even its brevity, as well as the risk of an unknown author, made it impossible for a publisher to accept it at the time when she longed ardently to see it in print. There is a wall between Angria and *The Professor*, although such motifs as that of the two brothers rise from the submerged kingdom.

Between this novel and its successor, Charlotte's love for her father was strengthened by his need of her. She was with him in Manchester during the operation on his eyes—a terrifying ordeal in those days—stayed with him through his darkness and, when he recovered, found in him a better boy than disappointing Branwell; this was a child who domineered over her and yet could not exist without her.

He clung to her because she was his eldest daughter, with ready sympathy for his neurotic fears. Each became to the other the all-important object. The comfort of this relation was impaired by a poignant fear of loss; endless were the lamentations, harrowing the anxieties of the future years, Charlotte worrying about her father, her father worrying about Charlotte in a dreadful reciprocity.

While her father lay in the darkened room, *The Professor* came back to her in Manchester and enforced her growing conviction that she, who was certainly not the woman beloved, had no claim to consider herself the woman of genius. That moment may have been as agonizing as the one in which she said good-by to Heger. In the depths of woe (absurdly embittered by anxiety lest the nurse suspect her of stinginess in the purveying of supplies), Charlotte found salvation in the projection of herself into a world of events and scenes which might be real although it was not. *Jane Eyre* (1847) subdued its readers by the terrific force of Charlotte's imagination. Many of the characters came from Angria; Rochester was a humanized Zamorna capable of love and chivalry; the proud sisters and Miss Temple were transferences. It is possible that Cecile Varens was once Caroline Vernon, although the weakness of Charlotte's early characterization makes it unwise to attempt complete identification; the points of similarity were externals such as their initials, their illegitimacy, and the hint that the mother in each case was an actress. The Reed family has been attributed to Charlotte's infantile Dunallys, but the principal resemblances between them lie in the bad tempers of Mrs. Reed and Mrs. Dunally and the similar number of children.

Charlotte's achievement lay in her successful fusion of unbridled fantasy with lawful imagination. She had abandoned an amoral attitude and had subjected her characters to standards which a large number of the reading public would find acceptable. The theme was still the struggle between the sexes, but it was conducted under recognized rules. The motif of revenge persisted, and Charlotte could not conceal her glee when told that a party of clergymen had instantly connected Mr. Brocklehurst with Mr. Carus Wilson. In regard to characters inspired by living people she continued naïve, protesting that she had not expected them to be recognized; but, when they were, she was unable to conceal her sense of triumph.

Her brief incursions into a larger society were of little use in her novels. The sources for those which followed *Jane Eyre* lay in her own active past and in the fading scenes of Angria. After her emergence from her infernal world, she seems to have made every effort to bar the gates behind her. Branwell's dreadful death was like a drawn sword before those portals. He had lived and died in fantasy and much of what she had predicted for Zamorna and Henry Hastings had been his destiny. The Angrian gates were closed, but now and then a bodiless emanation rose from the nether world, assumed a human form, and ranged himself with other humans. The Moores, the Ellins were of the stuff of dreams.

After Branwell's death, fear was for many months her daily bread. She was the first of the sisters to fall ill; she was sure she must have died had it not been for Emily's and Anne's tender nursing. When she rose from her bed, it was her turn to tend the sick; Emily had not left the house since their brother had been carried out of it. But Emily would not be nursed: the glimpses she had caught of the real world had never charmed her; Emily's home was elsewhere. She had chosen a better country than Angria: it was inhabited by a race of cruel but not ignoble Titans. She too was cruel: ignoring her sisters' misery, she was resolved to die and go to her own place.

It has been said that the mournful preface to *Wuthering Heights* proved that Charlotte was incapable of understanding Emily. Readers of the wild and whirling cycles of the *juvenilia* will scarcely hold to that opinion. Charlotte was once as barbaric as Emily, but it was in her to conform. Whatever she did for her sisters had its inception in love and loyalty. As she had written: "Natural affection is a thing never rooted out where it has once really existed." She conceived of two duties which she must perform for Emily; she must explain her work in a fashion which would make it acceptable to the real world; she would then provide Emily with a happier life.

There was nothing she could do for Branwell's worthless writings, but she could perhaps mitigate the harsh judgment of society and revenge his ruin by punishing the lady with whom he had been in love. Charlotte's imagination made her a terrific force in the actual world, whenever she cared to be. A few words, spoken as if in quiet sorrow to sympathetic Mrs. Gaskell, provided a posthumous vengeance on the woman who had, she believed, seduced her brother.

In Charlotte's "infernal world" the stone parsonage was wreathed with roses and crimson carpets made it warm within. Now the flowers of her heart were withered and the damp of the grave seeped through. Within her memory there had been six deaths in the house and Anne was preparing to follow Emily. Anne, like her mother, was a timid Christian. She said she did not wish to die but, if it must be so, she hoped for God's mercy. Charlotte had foreshadowed the fatal procrastination of the Brontës in *The Spell* where Zamorna lay raving for three days before a doctor was summoned. Even in that period and in that remote situation, the present delay in consulting a physician was peculiar. Mr. Brontë had energetically fought to save his wife, and Mr. Nicholls, not content with a local practitioner, would send to the best man in Bradford for Charlotte, but Branwell, Emily, and Anne were treated with the extreme of fatalism. Charlotte alone could exert force upon outward circumstance, but perhaps was powerless in the face of Branwell's madness, Emily's opposition, and Anne's meek acceptance of her fate.

Anne was buried at Scarborough. Ellen said sweetly that Charlotte thought it well "to lay the flower in the place where it had fallen." The surviving sister did not believe that Anne's work deserved to be perpetuated, and contented herself with explaining that Branwell's conduct was the reason why innocent Anne knew so much about sin. But long before Branwell showed signs of degeneration, the "infernal world" must have puzzled and distressed the gentle girl who had played "Gondals" to oblige Emily.

The composition of *Shirley* (1849) was far advanced when Emily died, and Charlotte determined to make her book a memorial to her sister. The decision necessitated the introduction of a second young man, and the insubstantial figure of Louis Moore emerged like a pillar of cloud from the Angrian kingdom. Most of the other characters in the novel were easily traced to living models—a process which in this instance exasperated Charlotte as much as it pleased her. She wrote waspishly to Ellen, "Since you say you could recognize the originals of all except the heroines, pray whom did you suppose the two Moores to represent?" We have Charlotte's word for Shirley, and Caroline was generally referred to Ellen, although Anne is equally probable. As to the afflicted curates, not a doubt was possible. Charlotte's publishers implored her to spare them, but they had angered her—on ironing day—and she was implacable.

Charlotte's most ingenious apologist must find it difficult to explain away her dislike of children. Mrs. Pryor's excuse for her shocking neglect of Caroline showed a complete blank in Charlotte's comprehension of human relations. How indifferently she wrote of child factory hands: "Let us hope they have enough to eat; it would be a pity were it otherwise"! Her cold dislike of little Cecile Varens has necessitated changes in versions for stage and screen. Lucy Snowe turns to ice in her appraisal of Polly's service of her adored father. Charlotte was no less hostile to children in real life. When the illness of a friend's baby interfered with her plans, she decided, on the ground of her own inconvenience, that there was nothing wrong with the child. She was herself afraid of death, but she wrote Ellen that it would be a good thing if a certain delicate child should die. She was caustic about Thackeray's nice little daughters, and the familiar compliments to Mrs. Gaskell's girls sound artificial. But the *juvenilia* show that Charlotte did not always dislike children, but regarded the princely baby in *The Spell* with tenderness and found the Duke's children charming. The change did not arise from her troubles with ill-mannered pupils: the well-behaved girls of Miss Wooler's school were as obnoxious to her as Sidgwicks, Whites, and Belgians. Charlotte, a literary artist, hated anyone who interfered between her and her creative work; it happened that children and curates were the chief offenders.

When Charlotte wrote *Villette* (1853), her love for M. Heger had become "emotion recollected in tranquility." As a result Paul Emanuel is a superb portrayal of a delightful character. But the wish to revenge her wrongs had outlasted the flame of love, and Madame Beck's portrait bears the smudge of an artist's thumb. There was no surer way to punish Madame Heger than to rob her of her husband. This Charlotte did in *Villette,* but she would not herself marry him, perhaps because she felt the union would be adulterous.

As if she feared that she had exhausted in *Villette* the material life had furnished, she attempted next a return to the old fantasy of the good and the evil brothers. "Ellin Hall" never progressed beyond its three beginnings. The second was a marvel. It had its source in her troubled youth; the narrator was a disembodied spirit haunting the house of Ellin, built over an ancient graveyard so that the dead who lay under the turf fed the flowers which bloomed over it.

Charlotte had come to the time when she wished very much to marry. Mr. Brontë was old. At his death another perpetual curate would take over the parsonage in which almost all her actual life had passed, where the Angrian tales and her novels had been written. Like the goblin of Ellin Hall, she was fixed by house, church, graveyard, and the moors.

Mr. James Taylor of the house of Smith, Elder, asked permission to pay her a visit. She expected him to propose and was ready with a refusal. But from the puzzled tone of her letter to Ellen, it seems incredible that Mr. Taylor offered himself. In any case he was going to Bombay, and Charlotte felt she could not leave her father and Haworth.

But if she married Mr. Nicholls, she need not leave the old house and she could be with her father for as long a time as the grim Separator of Brontës would permit. She did not at first recognize in the poor and unambitious curate the successor of the royal line of Papa, the Iron Duke, Zamorna, Sir William Percy, M. Heger, Rochester, and Thackeray. Papa said bluntly that Mr. Nicholls would not do, to which Charlotte assented, grateful because he had made up her mind for her. But, on further reflection, she saw not only the obvious advantages of the union, but a qualification in her suitor which had originally escaped her. For Mr. Nicholls was a romantic; for love of her he leaned against the garden door in a paroxysm of anguish; what better could Zamorna have done? Abandoning her "entirely passive" attitude, she allowed her father to see that he would not lose a daughter but would gain a son—and the daughter would continue to spoil him, while the son took the church services off his hands.

Charlotte's courtship by Mr. Nicholls proceeded with perfect decorum. According to the Victorian ideal, a lady was content with the simple duties and pure pleasures provided by her father's house; so, it seemed, was Charlotte. To marry, said the true Victorian, must entail a sacrifice of these delights: this the lover must be made to feel. Charlotte made Mr. Nicholls feel it. A lady must not love until her suitor proved his worth; Charlotte, looking like a "pale, wintry flower" in a white bonnet with green leaves, married Mr. Nicholls in a spirit of benign condescension.

But now that she was Mrs. Nicholls, she could with propriety begin to love Mr. Nicholls. The frail, aging woman adjusted herself to marriage with an ease born of finding that the demands of nature were more simple than those of imagination. Mr. Nicholls, if not the ideal mate for the genius, was an eminently suitable husband for the woman. Charlotte had given Mrs. Gaskell to understand that he was "very good, but *very* stern and bigoted," and the intuitive Mrs. Gaskell had remarked in other quarters that her friend "would never have been happy but with an exacting, rigid, law-giving, passionate man."

She had much to make her happy. When they returned from the wedding journey, she had the satisfaction of finding her father "not well," which proved his need of them, and presently "much better," because she was at home to wait upon him, and Mr. Nicholls had assumed the church duties.

During the busy autumn she wrote the fragment "Emma." The innocent Mr. Nicholls feared she was repeating herself, and so she was, but the original belonged to a period long before she had heard her husband's name. Although "Emma" was incomparably better than the specimen she had sent Hartley Coleridge many years earlier, it was a reworking of the same theme.

There has been a shadowy tradition that Charlotte's husband was in part responsible for her death, because of a long walk on a wet November day. But weeks had passed; Charlotte had recovered from the resultant cold, had entertained a cousin of her husband and paid a visit to the Kay-Shuttleworths, when during the second week in January, 1855, she wrote Ellen that she had begun to suffer from nausea, but that it was "too soon" to make conjectures. On February 17, convinced that she was pregnant, she made a will leaving all she had to her husband, unless a child or children should survive her, in which case his share would be a life interest in her little fortune. Exhausted by pernicious vomiting, she died during the night of March 30.

She died young. As to what she would have accomplished, had she lived, speculation is futile. This woman who said she would not sing, since she could not be a Jenny Lind, would not have condescended to become a mere contributor to a parish magazine, although she might, with hostility on every feature, have felt it her duty to teach in the parish school. She seems to have exhausted her material in learning how to use it. Her theme was love, with a secondary motif of revenge. Her mental processes were adroit, rather than rational; she felt, where George Eliot and Jane Austen thought.

Her war cry against male tyrants was sound and fury; in reality she exulted in the struggle between man and woman in which he was inevitably victor; when he had conquered, he would love his captive tenderly and she would obey him in humility until, in a fury of boredom, she would renew hostilities. Charlotte roused some sympathy for repressed women but offered no practical plan for their relief. On the subject of the dependent female, she wrote despondently, "I suppose she must do what she can," and, conscious of her failure to propose a remedy, added grandiloquently that, when patient industry had proved unavailing, "the sufferer is free, is entitled, at last to send up to Heaven any piercing cry for relief, if by that cry he can hope to obtain succour."

The *juvenilia* are important as a study in protracted adolescence and as a matchless means for observing the development of a romancist. They are also a proof of the practical wisdom of those writers who lay violent hands upon their own early work.

To know her was to love her
To mention was to praise

Elizabeth Gaskell

UNLIKE MOST VICTORIAN AUTHORS, Elizabeth Gaskell never needed to write in a desperate eagerness to provide for a household. Her life was unusually fortunate; there was always someone to take care of her. She could not escape all the griefs and responsibilities of mature life, but, as she had no special aptitude for meeting them, and was personally a very charming woman, she was able to cast most of her burdens upon willing shoulders. As a writer, she was at her best when she found her inspiration in what seemed, as she recalled them, the idyllic days of childhood and of youth. Money was something she thought of as a means toward a more luxurious, more hospitable way of life, a provision for charities which would be stinted by the narrow bounds of her husband's salary and their small private income. She was a very generous woman and longed, in her warm, impulsive way, to have everyone happy and good.

No doubt her prime motive in writing was the pleasure she found in self-expression: she enjoyed talking; and writing, according to her practice of it, was scarcely more laborious. But next to this satisfaction was her touching desire to establish harmony between people and classes who hated each other. She was a gifted but not a subtle woman; she saw that the social condition of the masses was horrible, but she had no idea of the complexity of the economic relations which made it so; she thought that if the workers could be explained to the masters and the masters explained to their men, a kind of spiritual conversion would take place and harmony be born of sympathy. As a novelist, she was betrayed by her zeal for reconciliation into much false sentiment.

Mrs. Gaskell was a true Victorian. She shared the general approval of self-sacrifice and felt a kindly pity for the girl gone wrong; she held somewhat advanced ideas of the responsibility of her generation toward that which would follow; but her chief ethical preoccupation was with the Lie in its various forms. It is possible that her interest originated in a belief that deception was the greatest obstacle to that sympathetic understanding which was her panacea for individual and class quarrels; but it is more likely that this obsession, this opaque spot in the limpidity of Mrs. Gaskell's charming mind, was the result of the scoldings and punishments of a fanciful little girl accused of telling lies.

Three of Mrs. Gaskell's five novels were designed as social and economic works, but today we think only of *Mary Barton* as belonging in that category; *Ruth,* the story of the unmarried mother, was, even in the mid-century, provocative of tears rather than reform, while *North and South,* a pretty love story, scarcely merits consideration as a serious novel. It is not by her amateurish efforts to solve social problems that Mrs. Gaskell continues to deserve our gratitude; it is by those writings which had their source in the clear fountain of early recollections—in tales of a past which a charmed memory held purged of all unloveliness, stories of a little town, of a grandfather's farm, of kind, eccentric people. In relating these annals, Mrs. Gaskell assuaged the nostalgia of her own mature life; and when we read them, we too escape from the present, and enter her lost world to delight in its tranquil security.

We have said that her life was fortunate because she had always someone to take care of her. Charlotte Brontë had no one but herself to depend upon until the last year of her life. Yet in outline the stories of these Victorian ladies have a resemblance: each was the daughter of a minister; the mothers, Mrs. Brontë and Mrs. Stevenson, bore many children and died when their youngest were babies; sisters of these dead ladies brought up their children; both girls lived in small villages; their period of schooling was almost the same; they were lonely as children; neither published in youth; they married ministers.

Yet how dissimilar were they in temperament and fortune! Very much of Charlotte's unhappiness and Elizabeth Stevenson's good luck may be attributed to physical causes; the latter's uncommon beauty, while it did not make her vain, gave her confidence in the approval of the people around her. From the first she was interested in them, so that she became observant by instinct rather than by training; she was enamored with life, much as she wished to improve ways of living. It was not necessary for her, as it was for Charlotte Brontë, to transform the fantastic images of her inner life into fit shapes for public consumption, nor did she, like George Eliot, need to remold painful forms. Life was too kind to her as a woman to make her a great artist.

The country-bred Elizabeth Gaskell (1810–1865) took a naïve pride in having been born a Londoner, although from the time when she was thirteen months old until she passed her seventeenth birthday her home was with her aunt, Mrs. Lumb, in the Cheshire village of Knutsford. She grew up there, loved and petted by her mother's people, the Hollands. Her father, the scholarly William Stevenson, had left a Unitarian pulpit because of a conviction that a minister ought not to be paid for doing what was, so unquestionably, the Lord's work. He had tried his luck in several occupations and failed in all of them until, four years before Elizabeth's birth, he had been appointed a custodian of Treasury records. Of his eight children only a son John and baby Elizabeth survived their mother. John had gone to sea in the merchant marine and, whenever his ship was in port, he visited his little sister at their aunt's. Thus Mr. Stevenson, who had started so very large a family, was left with none at all, and, quite understandably, married again.

His wife's sister, Mrs. Lumb, was in every way the most suitable person to take care of little Elizabeth, for she was well-to-do and had only one child of her own, a crippled girl who, during the rest of her short life, devoted herself to the small cousin. Mrs. Lumb's husband was insane and had been cared for away from home after the first year of marriage. It may readily be seen how important the newcomer was in that charming house where sorrow dwelt.

The Hollands, as well as the Stevensons, were Unitarians, the persuasion to which the Martineaus belonged; it was the most liberal of sects and embraced the largest proportion of well-educated people in England, although there were distinct social disadvantages in not belonging to the Established Church. These did not trouble little Elizabeth, who, surrounded by Hollands, worshipped in a very ancient picturesque chapel. Many of her relations were middle-aged or elderly, and the pretty manners of the little girl mirrored their sedate behavior. Dr. Peter Holland took his little niece on his long country round of visits, just as Mollie's father was to do in *Wives and Daugh-*

ters, and there were outings at Sandlebridge Farm which Grandfather Holland owned and picnics in the grounds of a great house where games were played and stories told and the boys rowed the girls on the moat; these simple delights were to be made immortal in such stories as "Cousin Phillis" and "Mr. Harrison's Confessions." When Mrs. Gaskell recalled her childhood, she confessed that it had been lonely; but when she saw it as existing in tranquil suspension somewhere in time and space, it seemed a piece of perfection. The observant, impulsive girl had then stored her experiences; when she withdrew them, they were not altogether the same, but rather what she wished them to be.

Elizabeth Stevenson was fortunate in her education. We know almost nothing about her early schooling in Knutsford except that she was taught dancing and French by a quaint gentleman who had emigrated in the Revolution, and who would make the subject of a charming little article. But when she was fifteen, her aunt sent her to Avonbank, a school kept by the four erudite Byerly sisters, daughters of the partner-nephew of the potter, Josiah Wedgwood, and connections of the Holland family. Avonbank was a great old house rich in traditions, among them the legend that there Shakespeare had written the ghost scenes of *Hamlet*. Long years after, Elizabeth used it as Hanbury Court in *My Lady Ludlow* (1858). The girls studied French, Italian, and Latin; they were thoroughly drilled in deportment and etiquette, so that Elizabeth's beauty was enriched by a grace which prevented her suffering from the sense of awkwardness in society which troubled Charlotte Brontë and George Eliot.

The young ladies of Avonbank school went in a body to Church, and Elizabeth's aunt was too liberal to demand an exception in her niece's case. The young girl was moved by the beauty of the ritualistic service, but feared that it was not altogether pleasing to God. During her last year at home, she had taught a class in the Unitarian Sunday School and might, had she been like Charlotte Brontë or George Eliot, have supposed herself qualified to take a stand on her religious experience. But she was not assertive; she was merely a pretty, well-behaved young girl. During her two years at Avonbank, she did not go home for holidays but was taken on various excursions into the country around Stratford; one of these furnished material for her first article, "A Visit to Clopton Hall," published some twenty years later.

Thus she reached the age of seventeen without having experienced anything worse than the vague loneliness common to all young folk as they begin to feel the pains of individuality. Now grief and a shadow of mystery descended: John, her elder brother, disappeared on a voyage to India; he and his ship were no more heard of in the home country. Elizabeth grieved very much and was especially troubled by the uncertainty of his fate. When she commenced to write fiction, she began the process of bringing John back to life: Peter in *Cranford,* Margaret's brother in *North and South,* Charles in "Strange Disappearances," the first husband in "The Manchester Marriage," are all answers to the unanswerable.

Her school days at Avonbank over, she returned to Aunt Lumb's tranquil house. But her stay there was brief, for the father, of whom she had seen little, sent for her to join him in London. The loss of his oldest child had deeply grieved him, and his health had given way. The second Mrs. Stevenson had two children, a half-brother and a half-sister for Elizabeth. The impulsive girl took a dislike to her stepmother, who, in her opinion, was not making her father happy. This led to one of the few instances where Elizabeth Gaskell used her art as an instrument of punishment; Mrs. Stevenson became the stepmother of *Wives and Daughters*. Victorian readers were shocked at Clare's duplicity and probably Mrs. Gaskell shared their horror, but to us Clare seems so pretty, so little harmful in her passing fits of pique, so genuinely sure that she, herself, is amiable, unselfish, and long-suffering, that we are not disposed to judge her harshly.

Some jealous pangs endured by Mrs. Stevenson should be forgiven her. Her husband was absorbed in his recovered daughter, whose future worried him while her presence charmed. He predicted gloomily that she would have to go out as a governess, since he would have nothing to leave her. This dire foreboding had the happiest result, for realizing that the better qualifications she possessed the more probable her success in the profession, he spent the remaining two years of his life in teaching her. His sound scholarship, his interest in research, he could not impart; but he could cultivate her facile intelligence until she seemed as wise as any pretty girl of nineteen had right and reason to be. Mr. Stevenson suffered a stroke of paralysis, and for the remaining months of his life, Elizabeth was not only pupil but nurse. She had grown exceedingly fond of the father from whom she had long been separated, and, because he was in so great measure a new friend, saw him with an objectivity impossible to most daughters. The relation between stately Margaret and Mr. Hale in *North and South* was a transcription from that of Elizabeth and Mr. Stevenson.

During the two years which followed her father's death in March, 1829, Elizabeth had no settled home, but the situation, which in most cases would have been deplorable, was in hers a time for travel and for broadening experience. Much of it was spent with the daughter of a Unitarian minister, the excellent Ann Turner, the young lady who years before had convinced little Harriet Martineau that a mother who sat up late to do her daughter's mending might be presumed to love her. In the great cholera scare Ann and Elizabeth were sent to Edinburgh for safety; Elizabeth would make use of the lonely months spent in the north for the framework of her charming *Round the Sofa*. As yet, she was not, so far as we know, even keeping a diary, but her memory was her alchemist's crucible.

From Scotland she accompanied Miss Turner to Manchester, to the home of Ann's sister, whose husband, like their father, was a minister. His assistant at the Cross Street Unitarian Chapel was William Gaskell, a tall, slender young man with a thin, humorous face. He was a scholar but of a more practical cast than Mr. Stevenson. A Master of Arts from Glasgow University, he had studied theology in Manchester College. The stipend from the Chapel was small, but his father was able to make him an allowance which put him in a position to marry. The beautiful, vivacious Elizabeth and the serious, kind young minister loved each other and were married after a brief engagement. No more suitable marriage could have been imagined; both were independent of family ties, they were intellectuals and Unitarians, young and hopeful. William Gaskell's position was excellent, even in a worldly sense, for the congregation of Cross Street Chapel was wealthy and fashionable; on a Sunday morning thirty carriages waited in the street for the conclusion of the service. Elizabeth's life had been passed among Dissenters, and the fact that she and William could not be legally married by Ann's father or brother-in-law or even within Cross Street Chapel was too familiar to seem a trouble.

She went to her old home in Knutsford, where her aunt provided the dowry and set the wedding breakfast. The wedding day was August 30, 1832, the year of the Reform Bill. Her uncle, the doctor, gave the bride away, and, because she was a favorite, the villagers strewed the ground with pure white sand and decorated it with drawings of flowers and the traditional verses:

> Long may they live,
> Happy may they be,
> And blessed with a numerous
> Pro-gen-y.

The ancient good luck wishes would be fulfilled. The bride was to live on for thirty-three years and bear six children, of whom four daughters would survive their mother; William's green old age would end fifty-two years from that morning; in the end they were to lie side by side in the Chapel yard at Knutsford.

He had a month's holiday from the Manchester parish, which the young people spent in Wales. Elizabeth treasured the memory of valley and hill and, in her lavish way, lent the happy corner to the unmarried lovers in *Ruth*.

William brought home the bride on her twenty-second birthday. He had married a born housekeeper who had been trained in domestic matters by Aunt Lumb. It is probable that of the two professions, housekeeping and writing, Mrs. Gaskell preferred the former, where results are speedy and nervous tension finds a quick relief. She remembered what the new corner house was costing William, £32 per annum, and, when years later she settled the Hales of *North and South* in Manchester, she allotted to Mr. Hale the same house with a £2 reduction in rental because the owner refused to redecorate. As time passed and the bride grew into the matron and mother, she trained her maids with kindly rigor, supervised the butter-making and the salting down of meat, lived a courteous reproach to less accomplished ladies.

The bride's energy was inexhaustible. Naturally the well-to-do of the congregation wished to entertain the young folk, and there were many wearisome tea-drinkings in the homes of Manchester "masters." But William cared a great deal about the "hands" of the huge town, even those who never came to hear him preach. He and his wife, sometimes together, often singly, visited the poor and did what they could to relieve their chronic misery. Her activity was greater than her strength, and her baby was born dead in the summer after her marriage.

The years which followed were full of such incidents as befell Victorian families of the upper middle class; several children were born; the motherly aunt died and was greatly missed, but the money she left eased the business of living; an increase in William's salary made it possible for him to take his wife to the Continent for a holiday. There they met William and Mary Howitt and heard from those experienced authors that Elizabeth had an unmistakable flair for writing.

William might have felt that, if the family must produce an author, he should be the one. He was a scholar and a gifted preacher; he might have published a book of sermons and made Sunday afternoon duller than ever in English households. Nobly, he wrote little and encouraged his wife to write much. They began as partners, collaborating in a poem which was published in *Blackwood's Edinburgh Magazine,* January, 1837; he continued to help her in unobtrusive ways. He put his exhaustive knowledge of the Lancashire dialect at her disposal; he found appropriate verses for chapter headings and, when he could not find them, composed the wanted lines, not always happily; he brought home odd items from his pastoral calls, material which she could furbish forth as short stories. As he grew older, he developed a comfortable interest in crime and studied the newspapers in search of gruesome episodes. But even better than these demonstrations were his rocklike confidence in her ability and his assurance that it was not wrong for her to spend her time writing. As a minister he possessed a study, but she wrote in a dining room with three doors. She chose to have it thus; probably her intense interest in household affairs would have made it difficult for her to concentrate in seclusion.

Mr. Howitt published the account of her visit to Clopton Hall as the work of "a fair correspondent." He did not pay her, but even if he had done so, even if her eyes had been dazzled by the sight of her name in print, she could have written little during the next four years. In the autumn of 1842, she had a fourth little daughter, and in that of 1843, a first son, William, after his father and grandfather. He was too small to call by such a dignified name and while he lived—not quite a year—he was their baby Willy.

Mrs. Gaskell was a sensible, affectionate mother to her girls, exhibiting toward them the eminent practicality with which she managed her household, but her infant son was her heart's love and when his brief, endearing visit was over her grief almost destroyed her. Her usually happy temper had no power to sustain misfortune; this was a burden no one else could bear, and she was long ill and despairing. Yet she did not feel that she was peculiarly afflicted; realizing that her baby had been cared for with the utmost tenderness, she could lavish pity upon a laboring man, who asked her in his desperation if she had ever seen a child starved to death; thus she learned to blend her own pain with that of the swarming poor of Manchester.

The anxious husband attempted to rouse her from her passive contemplation of suffering; he suggested that she begin writing, not an article, but a story. It is probable that her first attempt was the commencement of the book which later became *Sylvia's Lovers*. It was, of all her novels, her own favorite, and is the only one which carries a dedication. The words, "To my dear husband by her who best knows his value," are suggestive of sorrow shared and gratitude for unfailing sympathy.

She may have put *Sylvia's Lovers* aside because of her unconscious longing to merge her loss in the woeful stream of Manchester; the abandoned story was a romantic tragedy with no special significance for the mid-century, while *Mary Barton* (1848) is a social novel in which the characters are subject to their hostile environment and the love interest is subordinated to the economic situation. It bears the merits and the defects of a work resulting from a didactic purpose.

In the ethical sense it was a needed book. By adoption, Mrs. Gaskell was a Manchester woman; the suffering of the underprivileged, the mutual hatred and suspicion between classes had for fifteen years been bound up in her bundle of life. She was under the influence of a husband who was deeply interested in adult education and in the training of young men. But there were other gifted women in England who would not have been roused to humanitarian efforts by these incentives. It was Elizabeth's Gaskell's overflowing sympathy which made her see both sides of the labor question and pity oppressor and oppressed. There was, of course, danger in this superabundance of good feeling, but if she was often sentimental, she was never silly.

Her sense of parental responsibility was unusual in Victorian times. Parents who considered birth control a monstrous sin were not inclined to feel they had incurred a debt to their children by bringing them into the world; the debt, to their minds, was on the part of the offspring. But Mrs. Gaskell, although doubtless shocked at the idea of evading motherhood, did feel that the adult population was answerable for the next generation and quailed before the prospect of pallid babies growing up to perpetuate the class struggle.

If she had begun her career with a domestic novel, she might have written a much better book without making any impression on a public reveling in the strong scenes of Dickens and thrilled by the recent *Jane Eyre*. The theme of *Mary Barton,* the singular sincerity of tone, and its sensational scenes appealed to the reforming spirit in clerical and literary circles. Mrs. Gaskell had been a considerable time in writing her book and a year passed between its completion and its appearance, although Mrs. Browning's uncharitable supposition that most publishers had refused it was erroneous. Following the Victorian custom of adopting a masculine pseudonym, she chose the peculiarly ugly "Cotton Mather Mills," but soon laid aside this harsh and unimaginative name for "Mrs. Gaskell." Victorian matrons who wrote without deeper disguise clung to their husbands' names as the insignia of respectability—Mrs. Trollope, Mrs. Marsh, Mrs. Clive, Mrs. Crowe, Mrs. Gore, Mrs. Oliphant. In 1848 Chapman and Hall paid Mrs. Gaskell £100 for *Mary Barton,* £50 below the price which Colburn in 1849 paid twenty-one-year-old Margaret Wilson (Oliphant) for *Margaret Maitland.*

Any social novel worthy the name must be controversial; while *Mary Barton* won the plaudits of a respectable number of clerical and political reformers, millowners and their friends protested that the representation of their class by the Carson family was highly invidious. It was felt by critics that the number of deathbeds was excessive, and that the tragic elements should be relieved by humor. The author herself believed that tragedy and comedy should be put together like a layer cake, but her sorrow had made mirth impossible. She was always to be a singularly impulsive, natural writer.

The action of *Mary Barton* began in the "bad year" of 1839 with food high and work scarce, when the Chartists rested their hopes in the power and will of government to redress wrong. Mrs. Gaskell had read little on economics besides Adam Smith's *Wealth of Nations* and she could certainly not have compiled statistics or an accurate report on the subject of Manchester workers versus employers, but she knew what she had seen and she knew what her husband had told her, and could, with commendable veracity, present a series of convincing scenes. She could see the flaws in the proposed solution of the Chartists; their aims were so at variance that even if Parliament could be induced to grant their petitions, nothing would be settled. In the vital matter of child labor many of the fathers were opposed to the real well-being of the family; they wanted their young children to work, and inquired bluntly, How else were they to be fed?

As was natural in a novel of purpose, Mrs. Gaskell failed to allow her characters freedom of action; her enthusiastic backing of Jem as Mary's suitor was due to her decision that Mary must choose a working man instead of the flashy young Carson; she forced her heroine into an ultra-Victorian coyness because she could thus pile suspicion on Jem as the jealous murderer; an appalling instance of her author's interference was the maudlin scene of reconciliation when Carson held in his arms the dying murderer of his own son; thus she attempted to symbolize a union of labor and capital by the rapprochement of a workman and an employer.

Victorians were too accustomed to episodic novels to resent the fire, Mary's wild pursuit of her lover's alibi, or the really charming journey of the two grandfathers from London with their baby granddaughter. Job Legh had a place in the story because Mrs. Gaskell wanted her readers to understand that a weaver could be a naturalist; his granddaughter Margaret with her incipient blindness and her singing voice was a familiar Victorian figure. Young Carson, villain of the piece, was in the novel to tempt Mary, to get himself murdered, and in death to bring about the reconciliation.

If *Mary Barton* is judged as a social novel, not as a work of art—and this is the only standard we can apply—the high rate of mortality must be accepted. The scenes of filth and frightful poverty were pictured with admirable candor; the courage of Mrs. Gaskell, a country-bred, housekeeping woman, who ventured into haunts of wretchedness and dared to outrage convention by describing them deserved the highest praise. Nor was she responsible for every artistic blunder; it was her publisher who insisted on the long-drawn-out conclusion. And even the captious reader may take delight in various choice fragments. The references to ancient customs were charming: if the pillow on which lies a dying head is stuffed with pigeons' feathers, it must be snatched away, otherwise the poor soul can't die easy; a little child must live as long as he's in his mother's arms, because she can't help "wishing him"—she should lay the little mortal down so that God will take him up. In many a touching fancy, we see death figure as a longed-for friend. Nor was all humor lacking; two aged crones chat about women in industry; one of them wonders how Queen Victoria's husband would react if he came home and found "his missis to be away. Prince as he is, he'd be off to a public house."

A welcome change in Mrs. Gaskell's life followed the popular discovery that the writer, "Cotton Mather Mills," was in reality a gracious and beautiful lady, the wife of a Manchester minister. Gladly she made efforts to meet and know influential people and, going up to London, became acquainted with Mr. and Mrs. Charles Dickens, the old poet and social arbiter Rogers, the Carlyles, Forster, Thackeray, and others who could be useful, although it must be said that she was quite as charming to those who could do nothing for her. At forty, although a little stout, she had not grown less attractive, while her beautifully molded arms, bare when other women's were loaded with bracelets, her only ornament the brooch inclosing a lock of the lost baby's hair, her exquisite manners, even what Merimée would object to as her tearful air, impressed new British friends as indications of ideal womanhood.

Dickens followed up their acquaintance with a request for contributions to *Household Words,* which he was preparing to launch in 1850; it was not long before he was calling her the possessive and flattering, "my Scheherazade." It is not improbable that she wrote the story of "Lizzie Leigh," with which Dickens in 1850 began the publication of *Household Words,* before *Mary Barton,* as "Lizzie Leigh" seems a first attempt to deal with the sex problem, followed by the case of the prostitute Esther in *Mary Barton,* and rounded out by the heroine of *Ruth.* Lizzie, not yet seventeen, is turned out of doors by her employer when her pregnancy is discovered; her implacable father will not allow her to come home, but her mother's love finally reclaims the lost girl. However, Mrs. Gaskell does not admit that Lizzie's utter misery and repentance were sufficient atonement; for further punishment Lizzie's child falls downstairs and is killed. Nor do the survivors dare to lay the innocent dead child by the side of the stern grandfather; the little grave where Lizzie steals to weep is far from the haunts of men. Thus, a mother's love has redeemed Lizzie from a life of sin—in which Lizzie never took the slightest satisfaction—but her alienation from human kind continues.

The spirit of exuberance which had made Mrs. Gaskell attempt to subjugate London inclined her to adopt a larger scale of life in Manchester. The family moved to the pretentious house on Plymouth Grove which was destined to be the Gaskell home for more than sixty years. Mrs. Gaskell said, as conventional women do say, that the additional expense would ruin them, but she was privately certain it would do no such thing. She kept pigs and chickens, rented more land on which her cow could graze, increased her household staff until she employed four maids and a gardener. As everything went on under her direct supervision, it may readily be guessed what time remained for the literary projects which were to pay for the increased expenditures. Not that household management was the only rival to writing; in contradiction to her theory that a minister's wife was not obliged to do parish duty, she gave lessons in sewing, geography and literature to poor women, visited the sick, worked to procure milk for underprivileged children, and taught a Sunday School class of young girls. It was said that Mrs. Gaskell always had these girls in her mind as she wrote; this preoccupation had its share in the sentimentality of her tales.

But subject as Mrs. Gaskell was to current morality, she was perfectly independent of personal restraint. When she mentioned that William had "composedly buttoned up in his pocket" payment for her literary work, it is not to be supposed that William kept it there or spent it on himself. As Margaret Oliphant frequently observed, a Victorian woman was seldom a slave except on paper. Elizabeth Gaskell's earnings were her own and she spent them generously. She held stout opinions on her rights and worked so hard for the Married

Women's Property Act that it was popularly called by her name along with Mary Howitt's and Harriet Martineau's.

As she became better known, she ventured on greater independence in dealing with publishers. She refused to heighten the sensational element in her stories to the pitch which Dickens favored, so that, if it must be remembered against her that she was often bad, she was less so than he would have had her. She was inclined, as sensitive people often are, to be touchy. In *Cranford* she had mentioned the good Captain Brown's reading of *Pickwick Papers,* intending a little compliment to Charles Dickens, but he, not choosing this form of advertisement, substituted *Hood's Own.* Mrs. Gaskell wrote forbidding him to publish her story, but her letter is alleged to have come too late. Her painful experience after the publication of Charlotte Brontë's life resulted from her headstrong refusal to be guided by George Smith, who had warned her not to use her information on Branwell's love affair. When the storm broke, Mr. Smith did not know how to reach Mrs. Gaskell, who was pleasuring on the Continent. On his own motion he withdrew the book while Mr. Gaskell investigated his wife's authorities. When she wrote in her self-pity that the matter was "settled without me . . . for the best, all things considered," she showed no consciousness of her husband's and publisher's mortification.

Although she was extremely sensitive to slights, she was too impulsive to be always tactful. When she had been convinced that Mr. Liggins was not, as he claimed, the author of *Scenes of Clerical Life,* she wrote confessing her mistake to George Eliot, but finished her letter of apology with the unpardonable "I should not be quite true in my ending, if I did not say before I concluded that I wish you *were* Mrs. Lewes." Yet she knew that Lewes could not remarry. She talked about her large earnings with a freedom which may well have made her William uncomfortable; when she wished him to travel, she wrote to a third party that she could "soon earn the expense money." In Florence she called on Mrs. Browning and chattered incessantly about Charlotte Brontë, while the poetess sat in a silence which she had no opportunity to break. Such slips resulted from thoughtlessness, and it was a great merit that she was never envious of other writers. She adored *Scenes of Clerical Life* and protested disconsolately that there was "no use in trying to write when there were such stories."

The public had then, as always, an insatiable appetite for tales of horror. Some authors, notably Amelia Edwards, wrote them merely as a business, others partly for business but more because they shared the prevailing interest in the occult. There was a subdued morbid strain in Elizabeth Gaskell which relieved itself in the writing of macabre tales. As a girl she had heard many a weird story in Knutsford; as a young woman she had listened to Welsh marvels; her husband reported current murder trials and the queer superstitions he encountered in his pastoral work. Once when she was staying with him in a country house, their host, a magistrate, was summoned in hot haste to save a wretched old woman from being done to death as a witch.

Mrs. Gaskell did not need to tax her inventive powers in the stories which resulted; with such a wealth of sources, she required no more than a thread on which to string sinister incidents. But the fact that the origin of such tales was hearsay, not experience, made her unnecessarily diffuse in recounting them; some are spoiled by a silly piling on of horrors; more are injured by those reconciliations which her theories demanded. "The Old Nurse's Tale" was ruined by three ghosts when one would have been equal to the task; "The Poor Clare," a terrific story of possession, was dragged out to a scene of improbable forgiveness; "The Grey Woman," an admirable tale from a German source, a kind of spun-out "Robber Bridegroom" from the Brothers Grimm, had a disappointing surprise ending, an inverted reconciliation—the girl could not marry her lover, because his father had been killed by hers.

These ghost and crime stories were interspersed with moral tales on the Victorian theme of self-sacrifice, which give us glimpses of Mrs. Gaskell brooding over her Sunday School "scholars." In the "Half-Brothers" and "The Sexton's Hero," the down-trodden save the lives of the treaders-down; but as the narrators of both stories are supposed to be men, the fluting tone of the ultra-feminine Mrs. Gaskell produces an odd falsetto effect. A longer story, "Right at Last," is based on her favorite theme, the Lie. A servant blackmails the doctor who is concealing his father's criminal record from his young wife. As the wife is a brave and loyal woman, she tells her husband that she knew the family secret when she married him; she refuses to allow the blackmailer to prey further on society.

"A Dark Night's Work" is a longer, more languid presentation of the same theme, the Lie as concealment. A man dies as the result of one of those unpremeditated blows by which Victorian ladies frequently dispatched unwanted characters. The body is buried in the garden, and no one but the slayer's daughter and an old servant know of the crime. The girl loses her lover by dubiously inquiring of him whether it is right for her to marry him since a vague disgrace hovers over her future. Years pass while Ellinor in a dreamy, aimless fashion worries over the Lie and the body in the garden. The father who struck the blow has long been dead; the old servant is faithful, and at last Ellinor is persuaded to indulge herself in an Italian holiday. In her absence the body is discovered and the old servant sentenced to death as a murderer. Ellinor returns with scant time to save him. This was unmistakably a didactic tale, but it is not easy to guess what wholesome lesson it conveyed unless it be the folly of embarking on foreign travel when one has left a body buried in the back garden.

Occasionally a merit was made of concealment, as in "The Manchester Marriage," written five years before *Enoch Arden,* in which a woman servant and the second husband sensibly refrain from telling the wife that her first husband has inconveniently reappeared and committed suicide. Finest of the Gaskell stories of this genre is "The Crooked Branch," in which a woeful old couple are forced to testify in court against their brutal son. Mrs. Gaskell, admitting that it is not always possible to achieve harmony on earth, says of the dying mother, "the broken-hearted go home to be comforted of God."

Such tales of vengeance, remorse, and the unseen world, while satisfying public taste and the morbid element in her own nature, constituted the worst of Mrs. Gaskell's publications. Her only attempt at biography, in spite of inaccuracies and omissions, is a magnificent re-creation of a woman and her family as they appeared in the visible world.

The slight story of the singular literary friendship which resulted in the *Life of Charlotte Brontë* is in itself diverting. Prior to their meeting, Charlotte, the younger by six years, had formed one of her swift, foundationless judgments: Mrs. Gaskell, she decided, was like Emily. The ladies exchanged letters and books, and Charlotte, ever the partisan, urged Mrs. Gaskell to desert Chapman and Hall and come over to her own publishers, Smith and Elder.

The celebrities met first in August, 1850, when they were house guests of the Kay-Shuttleworths. They regarded their hostess with blighting indifference; Lady Kay-Shuttleworth had a cold and obligingly kept out of their way. Mrs. Gaskell pitied and admired the timid little Charlotte, whose daintiness charmed her into passing over the many gaps in her teeth and the irregularity of feature. While she listened to the exhausted voice as it recounted the wretchedness of schooldays and the family scandal which had killed Branwell, it did not occur to Mrs. Gaskell that the moral problem which motivated many of her own stories—the Lie itself—might be coiled among her new friend's gentle words.

Visits were exchanged between the gracious Mrs. Gaskell and the timorous Charlotte. In Manchester, the hostess herself practiced the Lie as concealment, when the frail guest said that a single leaf of green tea would keep her wakeful all night. It was a Saturday, the shops were closed, and in the Gaskell tea-caddy there was only black and green mixture. Mrs. Gaskell made no explanation but poured with a benignant grace; Charlotte drank without suspicion and slept profoundly.

Miss Winkworth, coming to call, found it difficult to reconcile Charlotte with *Jane Eyre,* a book of which she disapproved; but Mrs. Gaskell explained that her new friend's ignorance of convention was the author's sufficient excuse. She was not hurt when her guest, instead of going to hear William preach, set off by herself to Church. When at night Charlotte implored her *not* to tell a ghost story, her pity for the frail little lady was increased. Charlotte's own stories were eagerly listened to, and every word she said about Brontë affairs was accepted as proved. Her publisher's family had found Charlotte a difficult guest because she tormented them by analyzing everyone she met. Mrs. Gaskell, herself a novelist, delighted in such dissections. Her little friend spoke most beautifully of fortitude and resignation; referring to her own hard lot, Miss Brontë said that God had set some feet on a rough path while others walked the smooth.

Mrs. Gaskell was, however, somewhat selfish in regard to her new friend. It was not kind of an established author to ask Charlotte to hold back *Shirley* until after *Ruth* went on the market. But Charlotte, capable of extraordinary generosity toward those of whom she approved, had already asked Mr. Smith to give *Ruth* precedence.

Ruth (1853), whose ostensible theme was the "fallen woman," was actually motivated by Mrs. Gaskell's old favorite, the Lie. The early chapters on the orphaned girl, her seduction, and her anguish at her lover's desertion are very moving. Nor can fault be found in Mrs. Gaskell's treatment of the minister and his maiden sister who take Ruth home and encourage outsiders to believe her a young widow. It is Ruth's subsequent martyrdom and her apotheosis which are sentimentalized. For Ruth was only technically a fallen woman; she had been cruelly deceived and had no sense of sin. When she was told that she was wicked, she supposed she must be so, for she was a docile and respectful girl. All her speeches on the subject were rhetorical efforts uttered as Mrs. Gaskell's dummy.

The author was probably baffled herself by the normality with which the girl accepted the sex relation, and here was writing better than she knew. Ruth was in fact a natural young person who, under favorable circumstances, would have been a good wife, mother, and homebody. Her meek youth made it easy to cow her into elopement and subsequent artifice.

When her past is discovered, the novel disintegrates. A chapel dignitary bellows at Ruth; she runs home to confess her sin to her own little boy who, poor child, is the scapegoat. The minister and his sister are persecuted because, in representing Ruth as a widow, they have lived a lie.

Having thus reduced Ruth to a sodden pulp, Mrs. Gaskell inflates her into a saint; she dies of typhus contracted while nursing her seducer. Then Mrs. Gaskell, in her unquenchable thirst for harmony, softens the Pharisee's heart until he befriends the orphan boy. Dickens's famous *rapprochement* of Mr. Dombey and Captain Cuttle (1848) may have strengthened her faith in such spectacles, but underlying any such authority was her fundamental wish to simplify human relations. In her presentation of the seducer she was no more successful than in *Mary Barton;* her experience had not made her acquainted with fast young men. In both *Mary Barton* and *Ruth* she fixed upon £50 as the pay-off of a discarded mistress—probably having heard of this exact sum as settling a similar affair in William's parish.

In a casual reading the sophistry of her real theme, the Lie, might pass undetected. It is not the Lie, however, which causes the catastrophe; it is the discovery. The minister, modeled on the good Mr. Turner in whose household she had herself performed the duties of a secretary, taught Ruth and prepared her to teach others. The little boy was the source of very great happiness to the minister, his sister, the old servant, and the young mother. Thus years passed. Ruth's position was certainly precarious, but chances were increasingly good in favor of the secret. At last, in a highly improbable manner, the truth came out and punishment followed. Nevertheless, from a pragmatic point of view the deception had been worth the anxiety it cost. Had it not existed, Ruth's baby would have been born in the workhouse; mother and child would have been doomed to the gutter. Ruth could not have become a competent nurse, governess, and secretary; no one would have taught little Leonard anything except crime. And even when discovery descended like an axe, if Ruth had behaved less like a demented woman, if she had consulted the minister on how to tell her little boy the facts, he would have been spared the full force of the shock.

Charlotte Brontë, who, though a spinster, understood Ruth better than her creator, implored Mrs. Gaskell to spare her life. There were, however, only two courses—death or exile—open to the fallen woman of the Victorian novel. Dickens's Little Emily was dispatched to Australia, and imperious Lady Dedlock died at the entrance of the crowded graveyard where the father of her illegitimate child lay buried. Anthony Trollope exiled his troublesome ladies, some to little German towns and one, whom he greatly disliked, to Patagonia. Mrs. Henry Wood brought back her erring Isabel, minus her front teeth, to die in the house she had left—very temporarily—desolate. Miss Mulock reduced the fugitive Earl's daughter to imbecility. Mrs. Gore ostracized her light ladies from the fashionable society which was their Paradise. Thus, when Mrs. Gaskell gave Ruth the *coup de grâce,* she was in fact showing mercy.

The author was, as we know, exceedingly sensitive. Members of her husband's congregation, thinking perhaps that she had found her Pharisee among their ranks, professed horror at her immoral book. As a minister's wife, she had to reckon with their criticism, which very possibly meant more to her than that of her literary equals. Among the latter, Mrs. Browning, herself a sentimentalist, was delighted with *Ruth;* George Eliot observed mildly that the author was "constantly misled by her love of sharp contrasts"; Mrs. Oliphant, who hated everything connected with sex, wrote that it was "a great blunder in art to choose a fallen woman for a heroine."

Ruth had at any rate established Mrs. Gaskell's position as an English novelist. Dickens, who had been publishing her short stories, suggested *North and South* (1855) as a title for the book she submitted in response to his request for a serial. To English readers this conveyed the contrast between northern manufacturing and southern agriculture, and Mrs. Gaskell did her best to work upon this broad economic scale. It was beyond her powers. The manufacturer Thornton represents the highest class of employer, and Margaret the type of cultivated London girl whose parents' home is a parsonage in the south of England, so that she combines the best of rural and of urban England. A union between the hero and heroine would, Mrs. Gaskell artlessly supposed, symbolize harmony between agriculturist and manufacturer, and she hoped to make a better case for the manufacturer than in *Mary Barton,* where she had been accused of partiality.

But *North and South* turned out a charming love story, a Story for Girls, with a background of factory problems diminishing in importance as the love affair developed. When Mrs. Gaskell remembered her mission, she jerked her properties into action, but such efforts were brief and perfunctory, as her own genuine interest lay in Thornton's courtship of Margaret Hale, a girl very much what she herself had been at nineteen. Mrs. Oliphant, probably the best authority on the Victorian lady, did not believe that the rough, uncultivated Thornton would have attracted the fastidious Margaret, yet Mrs. Gaskell must have known the type which her impulsive, desperately well-meaning replica would choose. Besides, Thornton has no rival, since the fine London gentleman is too languid to suit the spirited Margaret. It is also to be observed that Margaret does not love Thornton until he has detected her in a lie, a point at which she loses her sense of superiority.

Those elements of the story deriving from Mrs. Gaskell's own youth are delightful; the weak but scrupulous Mr. Hale, who leaves his pulpit, is the image of her own father; she is the self-reliant daughter who treats him with a mixture of deference and domination. However, the old desire for harmony and her longing to bring back to life her lost brother resulted in the unfortunate introduction of Frederick. The young man has been concerned in a mutiny; should he venture into England, he runs the risk of hanging. Yet knowing this, his dying mother implores his presence and Margaret mails the beseeching letter in secrecy and haste, lest her father prevent the summons.

Through Frederick, Mrs. Gaskell introduced her prime favorite, the Lie, and that other old friend, the blow on the head which caused the death of an unwanted character. Margaret lies in order to conceal her brother's presence; Thornton knows she lies but accepts her testimony—a highly unethical proceeding for an English magistrate.

The claim of *North and South* to be considered a social novel rests upon such episodes as the suicide of Boucher, the death of Higgins's daughter, a riot in which Margaret behaves with more courage than sense, and the establishment of the diet kitchen with which Thornton finally conciliates his factory hands. There are six deaths in the novel. The prologue and epilogue of fashionable London life effected a spurious unity: the book would have been better without this unreal social atmosphere which Mrs. Gaskell, proud of being London born and confident through her recent triumphs in the big town, hoped would lend sophistication to her novel.

Not long after Charlotte Brontë died, Mr. Nicholls and Mr. Brontë invited Mrs. Gaskell to write the biography. She complied with charming alacrity and, protected by her obliging husband, came to stay at Haworth's "Black Bull." There in regal style she interviewed villagers and old servants. All her life she had been collecting stories, but she had never sifted evidence, and, like Catherine Crowe, she could believe everything.

Mr. Nicholls was a little stiff with her, but she attributed his excessive reserve to his dislike of "heretics." With courtly old Mr. Brontë she was at once on friendly terms. After returning to Manchester, she wrote many letters, had Charlotte's best friend Ellen Nussey to stay with her, then went to Brussels to talk with the Hegers. Madame Heger refused to receive her, but Monsieur Heger showed her the famous letters. Mrs. Gaskell has been blamed for concealing their existence, but she behaved as a Victorian lady and as a friend ought to do. When one reflects on the shock they must have given her, it is impossible to withhold admiration for the intrepidity with which she pursued her task.

The biography finished, Elizabeth Gaskell set off with a light heart for Italy, leaving her patient husband to read the reviews. When later on Mrs. Gaskell sadly described her delightful visit to the Continent as the height of her earthly happiness, she was not belittling her honeymoon with the excellent William; she was merely contrasting the way she felt before she knew how the biography would be received with the way she felt when she learned that Mr. Brontë's feelings were injured, that Lady Scott threatened suit, and that Mr. Carus Wilson's friends stood ready to demolish her reputation.

Fortunately she could blame William a little, because she had asked him, or supposed she had asked him, to read the proofs. Mr. Gaskell had already done much to save her, and the libel suit had been settled out of court. Mr. Nicholls, although not in the least eager to champion Mrs. Gaskell, did not intend to have his Charlotte's veracity questioned; his letters to the *Halifax Guardian* buzzed like a furious bee. To attack Branwell's mistress was so much out of Mrs. Gaskell's character that it seems certain she was laboring under a delusion imposed on her by Charlotte. Her own punishment was severe, but when the *Athenaeum* rebuked her in awful terms she had the consolation of knowing that her husband and her family still loved her. "One comfort is that God knows the truth," she wrote mournfully. This did not, however, comfort her very much. She said she would not publish another book in England, she wanted a house of her own in America, she would never again be so happy as she had been in Rome, and her girls must *not* let anyone write a life of *her*.

When she prepared her next novel, she took unusual care in preliminary work, going to Whitby in the early summer of 1859 to look over the ground and study local color, and afterward writing letters of inquiry, and paying visits to the British Museum. Not only did she try to master facts; she took anxious pains not to injure the feelings of any descendants of the characters in her tale, while she actually rewrote portions in the hope of improving them—extraordinary conduct in a nineteenth-century novelist.

The product, *Sylvia's Lovers* (1863), was admirable up to the marriage of the heroine to Philip. The characters stand out against the seascape, the low-lying town, barren farm, and dizzying cliff. Sylvia is a willful, pretty child not made improbable by the attribution of extraordinary gifts; the dour Philip is an excellent opponent for the fascinating Kinraid; Robson's execution is discreetly managed. Unluckily Mrs. Gaskell was determined to attempt further tragic conclusions; she wanted to see the Lie bear its bitter fruit and to insist on a grand reconciliation. Henceforth the characters became puppets. Kinraid returns; Sylvia, who has developed into a thoroughly provoking young matron, rounds upon Philip for deceiving her and declares she will never again be his wife. At this crisis, Mrs. Gaskell had maneuvered her chief characters into untenable positions from which she was too tired and too inexpert to liberate them. A series of incredible episodes leads to the deathbed reconciliation of the meek, uncheerful Philip and his bad-tempered wife.

The length of the Victorian novel was Mrs. Gaskell's great enemy. She had not sufficient staying power and was, needlessly, afraid of saying too little. Her happiest field was that of social comedy; her brightest source, her childish memories. In the satisfaction of her nostalgic yearnings lies the secret of her perennial charm. Her pleasure in the re-creation of lost images is reflected in our minds; her world, static and secure, becomes our own brief refuge from reality. It is impossible that she herself ever actually lived in the environment to which she transports us. Her memory retained only the gently smiling hours or those in which tears fell with healing grace.

The beautiful pastoral novelette, *Cousin Phillis* (1865), is the only one of the stories told by a masculine narrator without incongruity; in this case Paul Manning, a sensitive boy, is feminine in sympathy and affection. The reader must put himself in Paul's place in order to appreciate the tale; otherwise what seemed flawless to Mrs. Gaskell's contemporaries may offend him by its sentimentality: death from unrequited love is not a modern concept.

In *Cousin Phillis* the Lie as concealment raises distorted features.

The girl falls ill because Holdsworth has gone to Canada without confessing his love. Paul, who is sorry and anxious, tells her that Holdsworth has confided to him his intention of returning to marry her. At this Phillis regains health and happiness. But Holdsworth, out in Canada, marries another girl. When this news comes, Phillis has an attack of brain fever. Paul confesses his interference, and is blamed for her condition. In reality, Mrs. Gaskell was to blame for everything. In this gentle story, she was so determined to have everyone "good" that she hustled Holdsworth out of England and threw his hat after him in order to prevent his paying the proper farewell visit. Had he walked to the farm, as she would not let him do, he would have told Phillis of his love. Then, if he had married in Canada, he would have been a villain, which Mrs. Gaskell could not endure.

Yet *Cousin Phillis* is an exquisite idyll. A blunt servant saves the conclusion from threatened sentimentality, and Mrs. Gaskell was either too sensible herself—or too busy—to yield to the friend who begged her to add "a last scene, long years after." Such epilogues, perhaps derived from Greek and Elizabethan plays through the medium of husbands familiar with higher learning, were favorites with Victorian women writers.

Mrs. Gaskell's death occurred when she was on the threshold of old age, although as an author she was comparatively young. It is therefore impossible to know whether the sinister and sentimental strains in her genius were exorcised or merely suppressed when she wrote her final and most nearly perfect work, *Wives and Daughters* (1866). In this, several elements of *The Moorland Cottage* (1850) are repeated, such as the invalid lady of exquisite sensibility and the father who, although he likes the little heroine, is determined on a better match for his son. *Wives and Daughters* bears a close resemblance to *Mansfield Park*, which it surpasses in humanity; that Mrs. Gaskell never equaled Jane Austen in the somewhat acid elegance of her greater novels was due to the sweetness of the Victorian's disposition and the carelessness of her craftsmanship. Through both *Wives and Daughters* and *Mansfield Park* run the undercurrent of anxiety over the inheritance and the resultant question as to which brother is the better match; but the difference between Elizabeth Gaskell and Jane Austen is indicated by the former's attributing this preoccupation not to the marriageable Cynthia, but to her mother, the devious Clare. Cynthia is more vulnerable than Mary; she lacks eighteenth-century veneer and is more charming in her waywardness. Preston substitutes for Miss Austen's debonair Henry; Roger Hamley is the "good" brother, courageous Mollie is as devoted but more sturdy than weeping Fanny. Mrs. Gaskell's characters are more malleable than Miss Austen's: the Victorians recognized a greater variation in types.

Cynthia resembles another devious young lady: she is very like Lady Cecilia in Miss Edgeworth's *Helen* (1834), a book which Mrs. Gaskell dearly loved. Lady Cecilia means no harm, but she is afraid of her mother and of her husband; she lies to protect herself; she lies also in the hope of securing her friend's happiness; she too employs an innocent party in the disposal of a packet of damaging letters. In both cases the affection of the young woman who has been saved by her friend sharply diminishes with a growing sense of obligation. Mrs. Gaskell's characterization of Mollie and Cynthia far surpasses that of Maria Edgeworth's Helen and Lady Cecilia, and except for this suggestion of incident and character, she is more indebted to Jane Austen than to the charming Irish moralist.

The difference, however, between the never cruel Elizabeth Gaskell and the seldom benign Jane Austen is shown more clearly in the analogy between Mr. Gibson and Mr. Bennett. Both gentlemen have, under a misapprehension, married silly women; but Mr. Gibson's folly is due to a wish to provide his daughter with a sympathetic companion, while Mr. Bennett has been actuated by the desire of immediate pleasure. Each suffers disillusionment, but Mr. Gibson does not publish his chagrin, treats his bad bargain with politeness, and takes what satisfaction is possible in his profession and in the society of his daughter and stepdaughter; while Mr. Bennett holds his wife up to the ridicule of her daughters and indulges in sardonic amusement at his youthful mistake. In an eighteenth-century conception of life as static, it is horrible to reflect upon Mr. Bennett, perpetually amused by his own folly, eternally beguiled by the antics of the object of his contempt.

Elizabeth Gaskell died before the final pages of *Wives and Daughters* were written. The novel had been undertaken in conditions warranted to distress her mind and aggravate the heart disease from which she suffered. She had borrowed money from her publishers in order to buy a country house, and increased her anxieties by keeping the transaction a secret from Mr. Gaskell; she told herself and her girls that it was to be his Christmas surprise—although she knew that he always felt the greatest reluctance to leave Manchester.

In the famine winter of 1862, she had been overactive in relief work. Since then she had spoken frequently of the uncertainty of life, but had taken no measures to prolong her own. Much of *Wives and Daughters* was written in Paris in Madame Mohl's apartment. That celebrated hostess was not, like her guest, a famous housekeeper, but there was surely no reason why Mrs. Gaskell should stand up and do her writing at the mantelpiece. She was also furnishing Paris gossip for the *Pall Mall Gazette;* at midnight she would carry her article down the many flights of stairs to the street, put it in the pillar-box and ascend the tiring flights to her bed.

But, if she made no effort to prolong her life, she may have felt that she had already had enough of it. She had passed through all experiences desired by the Victorian lady; one daughter was married, another engaged, the youngest was nineteen; among them all they would look after William; there was money enough. Her beauty had waned, her body had grown heavy, but in Heaven she would be given back all her charms; there she would clasp again the lost little boy. Her manners had always been justly admired, nor did they fail her now: she departed this life on Sunday, November 12, 1865, dying between one moment and the next.

Es ist der Geist der sich den Körper baut

George Eliot

GEORGE ELIOT was not so fortunate in her friends as was Charlotte Brontë, who owed much of her reputation to Mrs. Gaskell's biography. There were women writers in England in George Eliot's time whose intellects were scarcely inferior to her own, but none of them liked her. Eliza Lynn Linton was jealous; Margaret Oliphant was half-angry at the glass house in which Mr. Lewes kept the great woman—no one had ever protected her; caustic Mrs. Carlyle was amused at the blunder of one whom Nature had designed for "the properest" of Victorian ladies, openly living with a man to whom she was not married. And each of these critics perceived a certain truth—that the conflict between the inner and outward existence of their rival was unresolved. "Her whole life and being were moulded to an artificial pose," wrote Eliza Lynn Linton, and added that this inharmony killed spontaneity and passion in George Eliot's work. Mrs. Oliphant, exasperated by the solemn grandeur of the published letters, pronounced her a stupid woman to whom a weight of genius was attached somewhat as the "burden of the Lord" was laid upon the prophets of the Old Testament. In this too lies the glint of truth: to weld woman and genius into one complete being was the struggle of a lifetime.

The materials with which Nature had endowed Marian Evans

were not those she would have chosen. In actual life, she could never quite bring out her ideal woman, although now and then sympathetic eyes caught a glimpse of what she had tried to make herself— as when she swept downstairs in a black velvet gown which made her appear tall, slender, regal, and yet appealing. But the efforts which failed to make her seductive and charming in the world of reality were eminently successful in her novels, in which she satiated the hunger of her passionate, sad heart.

She differed from other women novelists of the time, not in possessing any new, amazing quality, but in the greater intensity of her emotions and in her intellectual power. She was very ambitious, very passionate; her acquisitive ability was enormous; she had the great advantage of beginning her career after she had determined upon a definite philosophy of life.

In a paper written before her own novels she stated her opinion that where one woman wrote fiction from necessity, three did so to gratify their personal vanity. She did not believe, she said, that happily married women wrote unless impelled to do so by some irresistible hereditary or "organic" compulsion. Women who were not forced to write because of poverty, women who were not influenced by a silly wish to be noticed, wrote in order "to solace by some intellectual activity the sorrow that in silence wastes their lives; and by a withdrawal of the intellect from the contemplation of their pain, or by a transmutation of their secret anxieties into types, [to] escape the pressure of that burden."

Thus, a century ago, George Eliot indicated the sublimation of the woman in the novelist. It is very possible for women to accomplish the "withdrawal of the intellect from the contemplation of their pain" by such means as study, travel, the exercise of charity, the willing sacrifice which love accepts. But the "transmutation of their anxieties into types"—the evolution of malign shapes which thread their way through the narrow corridors of the past—may be most satisfactorily achieved in the novel. To punish, to reward; to make matters turn out differently; to be rid of ugliness and clothed in light—these are among the pleasant tasks of many mediocre novelists. But one so gifted as George Eliot could create an objective, self-existent world of such solidity that she was often deceived about its origins and supposed that the characters and events were not dependent on her desires.

Consciousness of inferiority came very early to the little Mary Ann Evans who was, somewhat late in the day, to become the great George Eliot. The tidy sister Chrissey, the blustering brother Isaac were the mother's favorites; her father's partiality could not compensate the small girl for the feeling that mother liked the others best. Isaac was older, stronger, inclined to be a bully. To please him was her highest ambition, but all her intelligence was insufficient to teach her how to do it. Once he praised her for catching a fish when she had done so quite by accident: the gardener spoke then of her good luck, on which incomprehensible blessing she meditated, as something above and beyond right and wrong; it seemed to be joy which came when one did not deserve it. In the adolescent phase of religious fervor which succeeded these childish years, the concept was mingled with that of Divine Mercy. After she had ceased to believe in God, she retained Luck—or Divine Mercy—as the something beyond justice which ameliorates human suffering.

The youngest member of the Evans household, although a well-fed, neatly dressed, properly instructed little girl, grew up in the atmosphere of injustice which perplexed many young Victorians.

Children instinctively desire a world of assured punishments and rewards; they require the consciousness of law functioning about them. Most small Victorians felt that they did not understand parental ways and that the fault was somehow theirs. Little Mary Ann was not only of an uncommonly dependent nature which hungered for approval and affection; she was also extremely intelligent. The sharp-tongued Mrs. Evans lacked the culture of Margaret Oliphant's mother; she would have thought that lady daft had she heard her reciting poetry in the kitchen; Chrissey and Isaac, though older, were far less clever than their young sister; Mr. Evans, who was an able man in practical matters, did not conceal his astonished pride in Mary Ann's easy accomplishments. An ability to learn and to reason gave her whatever power she had over the circumstances of her childhood. She used it to exploit her father, flying to him when she was scolded, flattering him by her partiality, being father's little girl. Although mother could not be pleased, she could be forced to take notice; feeling the importance of being noticed, Mary Ann made herself a little uglier, somewhat more untidy, hacked at her hair, and accentuated her clumsiness. Like all children she took delight in seeing people startled by her cleverness. When she was a very small girl, she told a new servant that she could play the piano and, observing admiration on the girl's face, supported her claim by furiously pounding the keys. But the clever little girl could not really play the piano; and pleasant as it was to pretend, she would have preferred the reality. She would rather be honest, petted when she was good and punished when she was naughty, than find her way by ingenious tricks. Much of the emphasis on justice in her novels springs from these young uncertainties.

She was her father's companion on many a long country drive.

Like Elizabeth Gaskell, riding with her uncle the doctor, she saw the world from the point of view of the traveler on wheels and was less intimate with wild flowers and woodsy walks than Margaret Oliphant, whose family were too poor to own a horse. George Eliot always preferred cultivated lands; the wanderings of Hetty Sorrel, the scene within the grove where Caterina finds her false lover dead beside the book, touch the heart, but in both cases we lose the sense of natural scenes and accept the symbols of the tortuous windings and grim shadows of human destiny. In the world of the actual, George Eliot liked kitchens; her taste in paintings was for the Dutch genre. Her own hands were employed in cleaning and cookery, and she took pleasure in these tasks, which relieved the nervous pressure under which she labored. She never objected to those methodical, laborious occupations which were scorned by women of less ability; she admitted that she had no aversion to copying her work in longhand.

These excursions with her father familiarized her with the talk of country folk. She listened to his conversations with the men along his route and could imitate every one of them. Until she was thirteen and went to school in Coventry, she too spoke a kind of dialect. There, sensible of the inferiority of her language, she evolved a slow, sweet, careful voice. But the habit of guarding against a relapse from lady's into country talk made her a little stiff in company. In this she was very different from Margaret Oliphant, who scorned imitation, and clung to the Scotch accent she had heard from her mother.

The Evanses were scarcely superior in a social sense to their work people, and Mary Ann had every opportunity to hear kitchen gossip about poor folk and their betters, the parsons and the parsons' families, and the gentry at the great house which Mr. Evans served as agent. While her hands were still a child's, their unconscious grasp held the bones of the *Scenes of Clerical Life*. Probably no one intended her to hear the grim story of her Grandfather Evans's end—how he tumbled into a brook because he was drunk and his sons found him there, drowned. It was a recurring motif in her work. The straightforward account in *Adam Bede* may have been designed to free her from its horrors, but if so, it was not enough. Maggie and Tom drown; Caterina's faithless lover lies dead beside the brook; Dunstan Cass comes to his bad end in the quarry; Tito is cast up by the Arno; Mirah broods over suicide in the Thames; Grandcourt is swept overboard. Drowning and oblivion merged in her thought. Water was a symbol of the longing for death: she wished Maggie and Tom to die, because only in the renunciation of life could harmony exist between them; but like an enchantress she wished to death the thief Dunstan, the false aristocrat who broke Caterina's heart, the sadist Grandcourt, and the plausible Tito.

There was another dour tale in the family annals; her father's brother had married a Methodist, a preacher in the days when the sect permitted women to hold public services. Aunt Bessy had befriended a poor girl who had made way with her illegitimate baby; she had gone with her in the cart to the gallows. Mary Ann was nineteen when Aunt Bessy told her this story: although she had as yet no expectation of becoming a novelist, she now possessed most of the material for three great novels.

George Eliot was a tolerant and unenvious woman; she behaved with propriety and even generosity toward relatives who had treated her badly, and put up with many annoyances rather than quarrel with John Chapman after he had ceased to charm her. Yet in her novels justice is spiced with cruelty. She avenged her want of beauty and of charm upon vain Hetty Sorrel, proud Gwendolen, and the parasitic Rosamond Vincy. Other women who were pretty enough but ineffectual were dismissed with indifference; Lucy is sufficiently punished by Stephen's preference for Maggie; Tessa is merely an engaging fool; and Eppie, only a child whose mission it is to reward Silas and punish her own father. George Eliot appropriated as her own a third and higher type of beauty; in Dorothea, Romola, shadowy Mirah, the outward woman is scarcely visible; here the endeavor was to make the body translucent, a vestment for the clear burning soul. The pride of Charlotte Brontë would not permit her to alter the heroines in whom she found herself; George Eliot, no more "realistic," believed in the power of intellectual beauty.

Convention forced Victorian ladies to look very much as nature made them, a fact which, however inconvenient to the unattractive, was of advantage to the times because it meant the preservation of the individual. There was, of course, the popular ideal of beauty which through most of the century was the tall, fine, handsome woman; but very few women novelists conformed in person to this type. Mrs. Craik was "willowy," Mrs. Gaskell, though beautiful, was not tall, pretty Mrs. Oliphant was a little woman; but Elizabeth Browning, Isa Blagden, Letitia Landon, Mrs. Archer Clive, Julia Kavanaugh, Charlotte Brontë were all plain, frail, undersized women, and three of them were cripples. It was not to be expected that all these delicate ladies would enthusiastically create buxom heroines; in many novels a refined, fainting-away, lily-pale maiden triumphed over the fleshly beauty and won the love of the hero. This type of heroine had her admirers, especially among readers whose families had recently emerged from the industrial classes, because physical delicacy suggested a definite removal from the manual worker. The English upper classes, who had no anxiety about gentility and thought it a good thing to marry healthy girls in order to have healthy children, were probably responsible for the more wholesome ideal.

But George Eliot, who at her best was a delicate woman with a poor complexion, did not create unwholesome heroines. She made them what she herself would have chosen to be; and it is surely better to wish to be handsome and healthy than to enjoy being sickly and plain.

Her nature was essentially honest, but, until she reached middle life, the surface was easily moved by the wish to please those whom she loved. When she refused to go to church, she was influenced by a desire to gain the admiration of her friends, the advanced thinkers of the Bray-Hennell coterie, but she had not foreseen the distress her action would cause her old father. She was conscious of a lack of governing principle in her life; in sad scorn she spoke of herself as a chameleon. Indeed her only sure support was her father, and when he died, she was speaking the truth when she lamented that part of her moral nature had gone with him. An extreme weakness balanced her extraordinary intellectual and creative powers. She was wrecked by the violence of her emotions and without strong mooring lines feared lest she drift from one inconvenient harbor to another. A woman with her proclivities, in the period in which she was living, could scarcely be respectable unless she made a fortunate marriage.

At twenty-four she had her first escapade with a married man. She was then staying in Devizes in the house of Dr. Brabant, to which she had been invited in order to have his help with the translation of Strauss' *Das Leben Jesu,* a project abandoned by Dr. Brabant's daughter when she married into the little clan of Coventry intellectuals. The host was a vain gentleman of sixty-two, and Marian Evans was a nervous, impulsive girl. No one knows the details of their folly, but it is certain that Mrs. Brabant, egged on by her sister, said she would leave the house and never re-enter it unless Miss Evans removed herself. The old philanderer, scared by her threat, let it be understood that he had given the girl no encouragement. It would be difficult to imagine a more mortifying predicament for a young woman in the forties of the last century. The memory rankled and became one of those hidden torments which would be removed only through the creative process. But her revenge in *Middlemarch* was not vindictive, nor unwarrantably severe. She spared Dr. Brabant as an ancient flirt and punished only the sterility of the scholar. When George Eliot with an arch smile pointed to her heart as the origin of Dr. Casaubon, she deceived her questioner but told the truth: she had succeeded in transmuting into a type one who had made her suffer. Her good taste prevented a photographic likeness and although Mark Pattison was anything but sterile, he was supposed in some quarters to be the original, probably because he had written a biography of the medieval Dutch scholar, Isaac Casaubon.

In her portraits of other scholars George Eliot was less happy. The blind Bardo seems a collector rather than a student; he accepts Tito as an assistant with a credulity which desperation does not excuse. Furthermore we doubt the scholarship of those two bright lads, Tito and Romola's brother, and distrust the quality of the forgotten learning of Tito's foster father, a skepticism which arises from George Eliot's careless attitude; she does not know these characters very well, but assumes they are able to fulfill the requirements of the story.

A second, more serious love affair in real life began when she was working on the *Westminster Review* in London, and living in the house of John Chapman, an exceptionally handsome and magnetic person, several years her junior, who had a wife and children and a bad-tempered, good-looking mistress, Elizabeth Tilley, living with the family. The large house was full of boarders, many of them literary connections of Chapman, who was at that time engaged in the publishing business. Marian seems to have completely lost her head over him and to have behaved like a girl in her teens. Normally, Mrs. Chapman and Elizabeth Tilley detested each other, but in the face of invasion they joined forces, as had Mrs. Brabant and her sister six years previously: Mrs. Chapman said inexorably that she would leave the house if Miss Evans remained in it. Mr. Chapman had a big heart; he was capable of loving all three ladies at one time—the useful mother of his children, the handsome mistress, the intellectual sibyl—but when he found it impossible to persuade Mrs. Chapman and Miss Tilley to accept the situation, he regretfully escorted Miss Evans to the train. While he waited uncomfortably for the signal for departure, he assured her of his affection, but added, with characteristic candor, that he loved Mrs. Chapman too—and Miss Tilley— "each in a different way." Marian burst into tears; in his diary, he wrote that he left her "very, very sad." On a later occasion when the two were taking a country ramble, he spoke to Marian of "the incomprehensible mystery and witchery of beauty." Again the unhappy girl wept bitterly. But even during the period of her infatuation, she did not lose her business sense, and when out of range of his attraction wrote him firm and almost snappy letters.

The affair languished and ended, but she could not forget it. She knew that the beautiful "Greek," as he had been nicknamed in boyhood, had never loved her. Her emotions had once more made a fool of her. Here was a fresh sorrow to waste her life, until she could transform it by the power of her imagination. There was a tale John Chapman told of his own youth—of flight from apprenticeship, a voyage to Australia, a fortune made and lost. George Eliot's *Brother Jacob* suggests a refashioning of his experiences. It is an unpleasant story, in which the idiot seems to symbolize the haunting past which no evil-doer can shake off.

Tito, the luckless youth in *Romola,* is a second and far nobler treatment of Chapman, as the pleasure principle embodied in youth and beauty. Marian Evans had seen him prefer his handsome mistress to her superior self; Tito turns from Romola to childish Tessa. In Tito's career one breach of faith invokes a second; cause and effect cascade the culprit down to doom. He is not altogether at fault as he slides from sin to sin; at his shoulder stands his creator, occasionally giving the persuasive push.

As for Romola, her conception of the ideal husband is that of a Victorian lady; he must be what Charlotte Brontë married—a gentleman who promises to take care of her and of her father, help the latter with his work, realize the sacrifice she makes in accepting him, and interfere with the old ways as little as possible. Romola, the Florentine lady of the fifteenth century, is strangely unaware of sexual passion; she does not object to Tessa because the fact that Tessa is Tito's mistress lifts a load of wifely responsibility off her own shoulders; she can forgive Tito for his infidelity but not for selling her father's property.

We have said that George Eliot had an advantage over her sister novelists in having adopted a definite philosophy of life before she began her career. Whatever the origin and cost of her repudiation of Christianity, it prevented her muddling in the misty ethics of other writers of the period. During the ten years before she joined her life to that of Lewes, she had time to think through her beliefs. Her mind was certainly not inferior to that of any other Victorian woman and she was associated with many of the cleverest men of her time. For her, this was a period of mental liberty which was somewhat curtailed when she left England with George Lewes. Whatever good she had of the union, she had lost the power of returning to the church of her fathers. She could advance; retreat was cut off. Even the "free-thinker" Eliza Lynn Linton said she was living in "open and admired adultery"; Charles Kingsley ungallantly called her Lewes's concubine.

She had once been an "enthusiastic" Christian; cause and effect, necessity, justice, are bleak monoliths to tower alone in a woman's universe. She was conscious of her excessive weakness: she, who could no longer stay her feebleness on God, was pitifully dependent upon man. Lewes, who good-naturedly gave her a Bible, in which he did not care to read, perceived how much her anguish at rebuffs, her dread of reviews, fears of misfortune, her too great dependence on himself were due to her hunger for God. This deprivation had a chilling effect upon her novels, and that "heavenly blue," Catherine Winkworth, was not alone in deploring the "utter want of Versöhnung." Nevertheless the definite views of life which she attained after prolonged struggle gave her novels an authority, a clarity, to which no "Christian" woman novelist attained in Victorian times.

The protracted literary apprenticeship during which she adopted a philosophy of life was not without minor disadvantages. In her early twenties, while she was near in life and heart to simple folk, she possessed the bulk of the material needed for the first half of her novels. The translation of *Das Leben Jesu* and the preparation of pompous articles for the *Westminster* were poor preparations for novel writing. In her forties she had become artificial. The schoolgirl had turned pedant, and a pedant who resented a show of scholarship in others: "Pedantry," she wrote, "is the ostentation of learning—no one likes it." Immediately after this pronouncement, she had the effrontery to quote from three foreign languages without translation.

George Eliot's liaison, although in the main extremely happy, had one unfortunate effect upon her novels. When a Victorian man and woman, no longer young, took a step so dangerous and irrevocable, it was essential to make it a success. Failure would mean absolute ruin for her, and, at the least, mockery and contempt for him. Lewes had a reputation for indecorous conduct; Marian Evans had previously behaved imprudently with two married men. The knowledge that the union must be indissoluble, that it must prove her absolutely right, intensified the primness of the woman and the didactic tone of the novelist. Among the audience to which she preached were Lewes and herself.

In most respects their union was as satisfactory as the lyric marriage of the Brownings. Marian Evans and George Lewes commenced life together on a basis of honest understanding and sympathy; both were plain, both had been badly treated by those they loved; both were poor and had very great ability; but Lewes had more to give, and the generosity of his behavior has seldom been equaled.

I have suggested that the reasons for George Eliot's turning to the novel form were those which influenced other Victorian writers. The need of money was perhaps the strongest, because Lewes's health was precarious and he had obligations toward the three boys and their mother. She was ambitious, and the slights and disappointments of her youth, the irregularity of her marriage urged her to prove herself so superior to other women that she had her right to an unconventional life. More powerful were those shrouded images which waited transmutation into harmless shapes.

The reception of "The Sad Fortunes of Amos Barton" (1858) was a revelation of the Victorian attitude to family life and especially to the lot of the faithful wife. Strong men, including publishers, wept over George Eliot's Millie; Mrs. Gaskell protested with tears that she had never before in all her life read anything so beautiful, Mrs. Carlyle confessed herself melted, Mrs. Oliphant compared Millie to her friend, wife of Principal Tulloch, who just after the birth of a baby sat up in bed to copy her husband's sermon; and, as far as I know, Charlotte Yonge was the only contemporary reader who had an uncomfortable feeling that the writer of *Scenes of Clerical Life* was not wholly sincere. Millie is really an extraordinarily touching woman, loving and gentle, imposed upon by a heartless acquaintance and unappreciated by a stupid and querulous husband. She dies, exhausted by overwork and childbearing. Twenty years later, her widower and the careworn daughter who has filled the mother's place revisit Millie's grave.

But perhaps Miss Yonge was right about these early stories; perhaps George Eliot was not being wholly honest. Millie literally dies from overwork; she has taken care of her children, of whom she has had too many, bound the books for Sunday school, sat up in bed at five in the morning to darn stockings, walked the floor with a wailing baby, waited upon an inconsiderate guest, and fetched the slippers for her exasperating husband. Yet Millie did not, George Eliot assures us, play the piano, because she never descended "from the serene dignity of *being,* to the assiduous unrest of *doing.*" This was surely nonsense, but it was not the only nonsense which passed the Victorian censor. Millie knew the parish was gossiping over the Countess's stay in the parsonage, but, secure in her husband's love, she left the situation to take care of itself; thus she allowed her husband's pastoral work to become ineffectual rather than give him a friendly warning, nor, in her happy confidence, did she give a thought to the loss of the Countess's reputation. Anxious to do her duty by that interloping lady, Millie provided cream for the Countess's dog, thus going deeper into debt to the tradesmen. Millie was too simple and good a woman to deserve to be blamed for these follies, but it was for them that the Victorians praised her. Nor does the thought of Millie's daughter putting in twenty years of hard labor bringing up her motherless brothers and sisters and waiting upon an incompetent and selfish father seem to modern readers the touching and beautiful reward for Millie's devotion which the Victorians considered it. The excellent Miss Yonge was not uncomfortable without reason; George Eliot had written her first story with a sentimental public bulking too large within her mind. At the same time we must take into account a woman's nostalgic, backward glance at the fold whose door was barred behind her.

"Amos Barton" delighted Victorian readers, but its successor, "Mr. Gilfil's Love Story," has a timeless beauty. Its origin was a legend of devotion; it was adorned with the romantic charm which the great house and the gentry had exerted on a shy little girl who used to stay with the housekeeper when her father brought her on his business visits to the mansion. There is something infinitely pathetic in the contrast between the gruff, kind, avaricious old parson and his own chivalrous youth; Caterina is a wistful maid in whom is no force of passion; her love, like that of the woman who created her, is a flowing away toward the desired one. Who would believe that she could strike her false lover a deadly blow? Her weakness wrings our hearts, as her strength could not.

"Janet's Repentance," the third novelette in *Scenes of Clerical Life*, has little merit for modern readers beyond its historical interest as a picture of the feud between High and Low Church in the early part of the last century. The Evangelical parson, Mr. Tryan, is the Victorian figure of a reformed sinner striving to atone for his errors while his life ebbs away. Janet is portrayed as a beauty in the grand style, but the puerility of her conversation and her timidity seem inconsistent with this description. Her love for Tryan is much like that of Gwendolen for Deronda: neither girl is conscious of physical desire. But if the principals are not flawless, there are a number of inimitable minor characters. The astounding vitality of Victorian novelists frequently resulted in an overdressing of the chief actors, while lesser characters, whom they saw in swift, sure glimpses, achieve validity. In every good Victorian novel, it is possible to mention a half dozen of these lifelike figures who play small parts in absolute style.

When these early stories appeared, Mrs. Lewes's equivocal position demanded the use of a pseudonym. Even after her reputation as a novelist was firmly established, the disclosure of her identity had an unfortunate effect upon her sales. As recently as in the early decades of this present century old ladies, here and there, questioned the wisdom of allowing young people to read the books of a bad woman. This effect of her union with Lewes is a little ironic, because it was her odd marriage which made and kept her good.

Aunt Bessy's story, *Adam Bede* (1859), rests firmly upon the impressions of youth reviewed by maturity and shows a great advance in handling and characterization. The haunting incident of her drowned grandfather is used with beautiful simplicity, and a tremulous music mingles with Mrs. Bede's fretful tones as she looks to the day when she will go to bed with her old man in his grave under the willow. Dinah is candid and clear, but Mrs. Poyser is a vixen and too clever, and Hetty is harshly treated. George Eliot insists that vanity is her heroine's mainspring and allows her no virtue but her sullen determination not to disgrace the family by revealing her identity. The only tragic figure is young Donnithorne, a prototype of "Lord Jim," the untried Englishman who believes he will behave correctly under whatever circumstances may arise. His suffering is more poignant than that of the not inconsolable Adam. The marriage of Adam and Dinah was unpopular with contemporary readers, although the union is permissible because neither is a tragic character, their parts being rather to endure than to act. Perhaps the Victorian reader suspected that George Eliot married Adam to Dinah in order to spite Hetty, whom she obviously disliked.

The third volume of a Victorian novel was always the most difficult for the author to handle and usually the least satisfactory to the reader. When *The Mill on the Floss* (1860) was published, there arose a storm of protest over the vulgarity of Stephen Guest and the drowning of Maggie and Tom. The objections to Stephen were for the most part masculine; with captivating manners, flashing diamond and seductive scent, he was the ideal gentleman of many Victorian ladies. The reader had been properly prepared for the flood and had been given ample opportunity to conceive of the bond between Tom and Maggie as the closest of which either was capable and to conjecture that their reconciliation could take place only in the very act of death. On the personal side, Marian Evans, who had suffered because of the breach with her brother Isaac, made her peace with him vicariously through the dying Maggie's with her brother Tom. The brother-sister relation, which Harriet Martineau in her anger at her brother James deplored as the least satisfactory one of human life, was for obvious reasons more important than the marital to most women writers.

The snow-cold *Silas Marner* (1861), which followed *The Mill on the Floss*, is an almost unblemished work. Its origin lay in her distant childhood, in the sight of a weaver trudging down the road, back bent under his bag of linen; thus the forked roots reached deep down and drew life from the days when she was a child exploring the world at her shrewd father's side. The characters were simple and racy. She had heard such talk as went on in the "Rainbow," and known congregations as narrow as that which thrust out Silas.

Ethan Frome bears a resemblance to *Silas Marner*, but bleak as is its landscape, hopeless the barren lives, *Ethan Frome* remains a work of sexual passion and *Silas Marner* is not. Godfrey is no desperate lover, but a young man in a predicament from which he must extricate himself if he is to marry a suitable girl. Nancy has affection for her husband, but, self-willed and prim as Romola, she is incapable of sacrificing her opinions. Little Eppie is willing to marry in order to please Silas and have a husband to help her in caring for the old man: this is again what Romola demands of slippery Tito, what Charlotte Brontë expected of Mr. Nicholls. The beautiful, chill book is a vehicle of a justice which smites the irreclaimable Dunstan in the act of theft, but works slowly and medicinally with Godfrey. Silas has done no wrong, and his chastening, like that of Job, presents a moral spectacle; although the thoughts of God are hidden from his understanding, he acknowledges the crowning mercies of his latter days.

Every author hopes that his next book will be his masterpiece. When two years later (1863) George Eliot published *Romola*, she was utterly exhausted in mind and body. She had drawn from other wells than those which had supplied her earlier novels; the study of history, exploration of the terrain, the experiences of maturity were substituted for the impressions of youth. She had been very thorough; English travelers bought the book as a guide to Florence, but this is not the best recommendation for a novel. Her husband had been ill in Florence and she was herself miserable and depressed. Although Mrs. Browning had written Miss Mitford that she "should certainly not refuse to receive" Mrs. Lewes, the visiting novelist made no attempt to see anyone but Mr. and Mrs. Thomas Adolphus Trollope and their little daughter Beatrice. Had it not been for Tom Trollope, who put his vast knowledge of Florentine history at her disposal, she could not have completed the project. He was very good-natured and very sorry for her, but it took all his not inconsiderable aplomb to know what to say when she drew him into a side street and told him "that she considered it a great evil and wrong that she had ever been born." Unfortunate and illogical positivist! Who did the wrong? Whose was the evil deed?

Yet noble efforts brought *Romola* into existence, and the woman who built a monumental work out of acquired knowledge and sealed up within its walls her torturing anxieties provided a grandly moral spectacle. *Romola,* conceived in sorrow, is admittedly a laborious book, but, if no character achieves success, none can be forgotten; and if the work is not important as Renaissance history, it is a valid document on the Victorian English.

Mrs. Oliphant, unable to report favorably on George Eliot's next novel, *Felix Holt* (1866), told Mr. Blackwood she would not review it for the magazine although the book was "exquisitely written." The general public felt that George Eliot's power was waning and especially deplored "the happy ending." But there was no more reason to make Felix a celibate than to bar Adam from matrimony; Felix is merely an enthusiastic young man with a talent for adaptation: the flaw lay, not in the cheerful finale, but in the author's misconception of his character. The triangle of Harold Transome, his mother, and the cad of whom he was the natural son, which would have fascinated a modern novelist, could not be further developed without scandalizing the Victorian public.

A gap of five years between *Felix Holt* and *Middlemarch* (1871–72) brought changes of great importance to the woman. A premature old age had its compensations in an emergence from her self-conscious awkwardness; her marriage was unquestionably successful, she had made a fortune, and her position in English letters was assured. *Middlemarch* was a much finer novel than its immediate predecessor, and in its measured and contemplative view of life yields a satisfaction to the mature reader which he has missed because of the obvious flaws in *Adam Bede* and *The Mill on the Floss* and the remoteness of *Silas Marner* and *Romola*. Dorothea passes like a rainbow down the book's inordinate length: on either hand are middling folk, mediocre in their fates rather than in their capacities. There is something soothing in this minor strain of acquiescence in disappointment. Five characters are transplantations from her experience, and as in *Romola* she herself plays the leading role. The public thought it a pity that she did not marry Dorothea to Lydgate: probably Charlotte Brontë could not go through with Lucy's marriage to Paul Emanuel because the union would be adulterous; it is equally probable that George Eliot felt a marriage between Dorothea and the likable Lydgate would dispossess the faithful Lewes, on whom the fantastic Ladislaw is modeled. When such intelligent

Victorian ladies wrote stories about themselves, they halted on the brink of the abyss.

George Eliot's last and most sophisticated work, *Daniel Deronda*, appeared in 1876. As a novel, it would have been improved by the avoidance of the Jewish problem; Ezra is a mosaic made up of a Jewish watchmaker of whom Lewes had told her, a dash of Spinoza, a visit or two to a synagogue and a very large tincture of Old Testament prophet. In Mirah we have no faith whatever; her long story may have imposed on George Eliot, but we will never believe it.

Without this apocryphal pair, the triangle of the Grandcourts and Deronda is admirable. If the young man seems a prig, it is not his fault but that of his disciples. Gwendolen's attitude toward Deronda is the unquestioning dependence of the patient on the psychoanalyst; it is a weak flowing out of love like Caterina's or like George Eliot's toward Brabant and Chapman. George Eliot seems to have felt a strong aversion for Gwendolen, who resembles her more closely than Romola, Dorothea, or even Maggie. It is conceivable that she might have acted as they did—Gwendolen, the most passionate of her women, she might have been. George Eliot attacked her psychological problems with wonderful acumen: Gwendolen will not admit to herself the murder wish, but disguises it as dread of "accident," or a fancy of "running away." Her situation is similar to that of Miriam in the *Marble Faun* or of the acquiescent son Ivan in *The Brothers Karamazov;* if there is less grandeur in George Eliot's treatment than in Dostoevsky's, it is lucid and English.

She was already fifty-seven. In her young days, she had expressed admiration for Madame Sablé, who, at an age when womanly charms invariably decline, was the mistress of a salon with "philosophers, wits, beauties, and saints clustering around her." And now she herself had acquired the most famous literary drawing room in England, although perhaps "beauties and saints" were not conspicuous among the guests. There she sat in her armchair carefully placed at the left of the open fire; now and again she heard the bell tinkle at the garden gate. Then Lewes, whom it suited to act as her showman, would escort the favored visitor to her side and she, the sibyl of English letters, would talk to him a little while in tones of melancholy sweetness.

But now the last novel has been written, faithful Lewes is dead, and on Sunday afternoons she hears no sound of the bell at the garden gate. She quotes a mourning queen—"Here I and sorrow sit" and her friends hover to see her die of grief. But why should a woman who believes that at death she will enter nothingness, relinquish this world without a struggle? Her frantic effort to renew life fails, she follows Lewes, leaving the facts of her existence to be woven into a tapestry in which the figure seems awry, the threads botched. But where the flat surface fails to record her finer inner world, the three-dimensional novels succeed.

Many love me, but by none am I enough beloved

Margaret Oliphant

MARGARET OLIPHANT'S STORY is known to very few. As she haughtily asserted, she was not given to public appearances; but the habit of seclusion, which injured her sales during her lifetime, does not account for the oblivion which has since enshrouded her. Length of days has also told against her reputation; there is always sympathy for those who early leave the scene—always speculation as to great accomplishments cruelly missed—but Margaret Oliphant, dying in her seventieth year, had outlasted a novelist's vogue and a woman's happiness. A brief wonder why so pitiable a story was so soon forgotten vanishes as we remember that the tale of passive suffering is not one to linger in the memory: Margaret Oliphant's misfortunes were singularly undramatic.

She was perhaps the most prolific writer the world has ever produced. Trollope's accomplishments bulk less large than hers, a truly prodigious output which engaged twenty-four publishers. Much of her most finished work was by her own wish anonymous. She was extraordinarily indifferent to her reputation, although her vexation when other women were ranked as her superiors indicates a scornful suppression rather than freedom from ambition.

Never a fortunate woman, she often missed happiness by a narrow margin. For example, a child destined to become a novelist would have been very lucky to grow up in the house where Margaret was born, a dignified, ancient dwelling within walking distance of Edinburgh. The drawing room boasted five windows recessed in the thick walls; through their greenish panes one looked out on most romantic sights—Arthur's Seat, the Castle Rock, the boughs of a giant ash—while a wilderness of bright flowers overspread the ground beneath. But her father and mother moved from the delightful house long before the little girl was old enough to be aware of the enchanting views.

Her first memories were of a humble cottage in Lasswade. Her family, the Wilsons, were Scotch gentlefolk who had come down in the world. The father was dour, the brilliant mother quick-tempered. They had two sons much older than Margaret, and the loss of several children, born between the boys and their little sister, had clouded Mrs. Wilson's life and made her fasten a crushing load of love on the children left to her. Willie was handsome and debonair, but had some mysterious "failing"; Frank was clever and conscientious. The brothers were exceedingly fond of the small Margaret.

Mr. Wilson would tolerate neither noise nor visitors, but, if undisturbed, interfered little with his household. Mrs. Wilson, who was pretty, pink-cheeked, and slender, with pure white hair, had a poor opinion of the family into which she had married. She herself was an Oliphant, a descendant of the Oliphants of Kellie Castle in Fife. Her father had been a rascal and her childhood that of an embarrassed dependent on her mother's people. She avenged herself on those who brought her up by exalting the side of the house from which she had received no benefits. Margaret naturally adopted her mother's views and thought herself lucky, not in being Margaret Wilson, but in her descent from the Oliphants.

The mother was a wonderful story-teller. She had a repertory of epics which celebrated the mighty deeds wrought by ancient Oliphants and their peers; she could sing ballads of the Border and had so much of Pope's poetry on her tongue's end that the Presbyterian Wilsons had a family joke: Mother, the boys said, was Popish. Besides, she was a great reader. With only one servant to help her, she was busy all day long, but, as she stepped about her kitchen or, resting, sewed for Margaret, she taught the little girl to read and talked to her as to an equal. The child had her own favorite seat, a stool by the open fire. Once, listening entranced, she tumbled off and burned her arm against the fender. The scar was permanent, but out of the horrid accident came something pleasant, because Dr. Moir drove out from Edinburgh to treat her and made her his little friend for life. Readers of *Blackwood's Magazine* knew him as the poet "Delta." He, of course, was acquainted with Mr. Scott, now Sir Walter, whom people called "The Wizard of the North."

Margaret's brothers spent the week in Edinburgh, tramping six miles home to Lasswade on a Saturday night and six miles back before dawn Monday morning. The mother and Margaret were always up to get their breakfasts. The talk at home was often political, on such incomprehensible subjects as Rotten Boroughs and the Reform Bill, for this was 1832 and Margaret was only four. She named her kittens Lords Brougham and Grey.

A solitary child, she wandered by herself under the boughs of the ash trees which met and mingled over the street where she lived; the stagecoach flew past on its way to the great towns; on a sunny knoll beside the swift river grew such giant primroses as she would never pick again. Her old nurse lived in a cottage much smaller than the Wilsons'—a "but and ben" as people called it. Margaret on a visit offered to read to her. She climbed on a chair, examined the books on the shelf at the bed's head, lifted down *The Gentle Shepherd*. She read to the nurse by the firelight, but the old Scotch body could have prompted her, for she knew the lines by heart.

When we remember George Eliot's fractious, illiterate mother and Charlotte Brontë's pedantic aunt, we may conclude that Margaret Oliphant was fortunate in her loving and gifted mother. But the child on whom Mrs. Wilson lavished her affection, who was the very center of her existence, never learned to be content with less. She was not spoiled in the usual sense, for Mrs. Wilson had a sharp tongue and a strong sense of duty. So far as she knew, she indulged her little daughter in only one way: the clothes she made her were as dainty as Princess Victoria's in Kensington Palace; since Maggie had no playmates to envy her, Mrs. Wilson could not see any harm in pleasing herself in her child's dress. The little girl basked in the fervid glow of her mother's adoration, and finding it poorly matched by the affection she received in later years, lamented with rueful laughter, "Many love me, but by none am I enough beloved."

In 1834, when she was six years old, her parents moved to Glasgow, journeying by canal from Edinburgh. The boat left before dawn. The little girl was terrified at the pinched look on her mother's face; it was there because Willie and Frank were being left behind. The morning cold was bitter; along Princes Street the lamps were strung like golden oranges. Margaret's little hands and feet felt frozen; she was frightened at the strangeness of life, of journeyings and partings.

At Falkirk, the Wilsons exchanged that boat for one which was painted red and green and had a stove in the saloon. Maggie's large brown eyes spied a penny magazine on a table and, as soon as she was thawed, she made a birdlike sally. She was very small for her age and learning was not common in those days, so that the passengers laughed good-naturedly as at a child making believe. Jokingly, one of them begged her to read aloud. Margaret complied with dignity. On the cover, she remembered, was the picture of a steamboat, for in the 1830's the Lords Brougham and Grey, for whom she had named her kittens, were trying to instruct the public as to modern inventions.

The Glasgow house was more pretentious than the Lasswade cottage, but Margaret liked it less. There were dark passages down which she ran fast, fearing a breathing something in a certain closet might snatch at her as she passed. Thick curtains shut out the light and enclosed the beds, on which lay straw mattresses covered with a layer of feathers. The mahogany furniture was upholstered in horsehair with "horrible webs of crochet, white, starched, and glistening" attached to chairs and sofas. Her mother scoffed at the giant sideboard, which she said was not "solid." Perhaps some dangerous creature lived inside; or it might be the "whited sepulchre" of the New Testament. The drawing room was dark of an evening because thrifty folk thought shame to light more than the two candles which stood on the tray with the snuffer sitting cosily between them.

However, the small resident of Glasgow was more interested in books than in furniture. The few pennies at her disposal would not of course buy them, but she could sometimes afford to rent one from the lending library. Her mother gave her freedom to read what she pleased and to go alone about the streets. As Margaret was finishing Bulwer Lytton's *Ernest Maltravers* with regret, she was delighted to find a notice of an available sequel. But when she scurried to the library, the old lady in charge was shocked at her diminutive patroness wanting so questionable a book and implored her to substitute a juvenile, *Fatherless Fanny*. Like most critics Margaret retained an extreme admiration for childish favorites; that she never found an equal to Walter Scott was not wonderful in a Scotch woman, but the high place she assigned Bulwer Lytton depended somewhat on the fascination he had exerted on the child.

When *Nicholas Nickleby* was published, Frank in distant Edinburgh copied the story, condensing it by a third, and sent it to his little sister in Glasgow. In later years the sentimentality of Dickens offended her, but this novel remained dear to her because of her big brother's kindness.

She had little of the child Charlotte Brontë's prying curiosity. Whatever was coarse or ugly offended her. Once in Glasgow, trotting along behind a group of girl factory workers, she heard talk from which she shrank back in disgust. When she grew up, she was not afraid of vice but affronted by it, and, like Jane Austen, refused to linger over shameful scenes.

Before she reached her teens, the Wilson family was reunited in Liverpool, where the father had found employment in the Customs. Frank too was working, but Willie, who was disgracing himself in his mysterious fashion, idled around the house. The men in the family were not regarded with the respect usual in the households of the period; Mrs. Wilson's love for her sons held a strong admixture of contempt, and Margaret was influenced both by her mother's attitude and by her own observation of their weakness. Out of this developed a great defect in the novelist: Mrs. Oliphant could never believe in a hero. Her charming young men are, after all, poor creatures. She treats them leniently and either spares them the demanding situations with which they are unfit to cope, or extricates them by a flick of coincidence. As a young woman her acquaintance with men was largely limited to her own relations; her grandfather had been so bad that his wife had left him, her father was a saturnine block, Frank was weak, charming Willie a sinner, and, when she married, her husband could not support her.

In some ways she became an extraordinarily fearless little girl. During a famine winter she bustled through the poorer streets of Glasgow assisting benevolent Willie in handing out orders for coal and food. The Wilsons were Liberals, and in the agitation against the Corn Laws, Margaret went from house to house soliciting signatures for a petition to Parliament. Her interest in welfare work disappeared with childhood. She became a very hospitable woman, liberal to friends and dependents, but not one concerned with general benevolence. Nor are any of her novels written with a social purpose.

The Wilsons neither paid nor received visits. The church and an occasional tea-drinking in its parlors provided their only diversion. Even in this isolation Margaret had suitors, for she was very pretty with a wonderful complexion, soft, thick brown hair, exquisite hands and extraordinary eyes, large and dark, with a suggestion of unfathomable depths. Her only defect was a pouting upper lip, too long and full. At seventeen she became engaged to a young man who was about to emigrate to America. He sent her dull letters from the land of promise; she told him candidly that they did not interest her, and in dudgeon he broke off the correspondence. Then the forsaken Margaret wept. The tedium of her life and not the loss of her lover weighed her down. She had never had a girl friend; she had never been to a dance; what had she to live for?

Her mother fell ill, perhaps with some nervous complaint, for the doctor forbade conversation. Margaret was her nurse and must always be in the sickroom, because Mrs. Wilson wanted to see her daughter, even if they might not speak. The girl, who like almost every other Victorian woman novelist, discovered in fine needlework the solace of mature life, as yet hated sewing and was tired of books. In her desperate boredom she began to write a novel. When her mother was able she listened delightedly to the story, which must have had some merit because later Willie published it as his own work. Margaret burned a second long story and then, at the age of nineteen, wrote *Passages in the Life of Mrs. Margaret Maitland* (1849), a novel which became fairly popular; Charlotte Brontë warmly recommended Ellen Nussey to give it to her mother.

The Wilson evenings were now enlivened by Margaret's reading aloud her day's writing. The family sat around the table in the center of the room and listened with uncritical enthusiasm. No one, especially the proud mother, saw any reason why Margaret's work should not be published. It was Mrs. Wilson's opinion that the ability to write at odd times and inconvenient places was a sign of genius; a body who hesitated over a word or begged for solitude in which to compose was a poor, feckless creature and had best lay down the pen. Like all her countrymen, Mrs. Wilson had Walter Scott on her mind; she knew the story of the shadow on the blind, the lifted arm, the finished page laid by; if Margaret meant to be an author, she would do well to imitate his industry and let the fountain of her words run freely.

Willie too had been ill. When he recovered, he told the family that he wished to enter the ministry. The mother's skepticism deserted her. Believing that Willie was "changed," she exerted herself to get him off to London, where a course of University lectures would prepare him for ordination. The obliging young man took with him the manuscript of *Mrs. Margaret Maitland,* for which he hoped to find a publisher, and as a result Colburn very shortly accepted the story. Willie was less fortunate in his own affairs. After a term at the University, he returned to Liverpool in debt and fallen, as the Wilsons expressed it, "into his old vice." Their reticence balks our curiosity as to the nature of Willie's failing; his long and pleasant later life in Rome does not seem consonant with any outrageous sin; perhaps Willie was merely indolent. In these early days his mother had not lost hope of his reclamation. Could he but keep another term at the University, he might be ordained a minister. It occurred to her that his sister's presence in London would preserve Willie from evil, while she would have the advantage of being in London when her novel was published.

Willie submitted with charming good temper to a sister's surveillance more strict than most mothers would dare exert. Margaret ferreted out several small debts Willie had preferred to keep secret and insisted that they be paid without their mother's knowledge. This was done by the simple expedient of not eating dinner. Instead of going to the table, the pair fortified themselves with buns and went on long walks, Willie guiding his jailer to many odd London corners. Both loved to linger over the little bookshops which in those days lined the narrow passages down Holborn way.

There were two cousins living in the house, Tom and Francis Oliphant, of the impoverished family in which Mrs. Wilson took such pride. Francis, who was an artist, escorted his pretty cousin to the National Gallery and was disappointed at the lack of appreciation which she was too honest to conceal. Her imagination was remarkably vivid and the paintings did not please her inexperienced eyes, which had looked for something quite different. At the theatre, too,

Twelfth Night grated; she had not reckoned on a fat, middle-aged Viola.

Francis Oliphant did not make a deep impression on the girl, who was living within herself rather than in London. He was then in his late twenties, by choice a painter of historical scenes, although his income depended on painted windows for churches and public buildings. From a very early age he had been active in the Gothic revival; with his friend Welby Pugin he had designed the glass for the new Houses of Parliament. Margaret's reticence in her memoirs hangs before his face like a veil, through which we catch glimpses of a frail, charming, and never-understood young man.

In London Margaret made a first friend. Where she herself was pretty, Gerardine Bate was inexpressibly beautiful. She was seventeen, a favorite niece of Mrs. Jameson, the elegant and indefatigable authoress. Mrs. Jameson, whose own marriage had not been a success, hoped that the lovely Gerardine would make a great match, but a year later in 1850 the headstrong girl married red-headed, bearded Robert Macpherson, a friend of Francis Oliphant, who lived in Rome. A mediocre painter, Macpherson obtained a papal patent for his invention of a technical process, and devoted himself to successful photography of Roman ruins. The Scotch families of Macpherson, Wilson, and Oliphant were intimately concerned with one another for many years.

The *Athenaeum* had commended *Margaret Maitland,* a book which we would advise no one to read, and Lord Jeffrey, then an old man near his end, had gratified the young author by his praise of her "pure, gracious, idiomatic Scotch"—which was doubtless all he said of it. Lord Jeffrey approved also the characterization of the child Grace and of the spinster bearing the courtesy title Mrs. Margaret, for whom the young author had used as models herself and her mother. The rest of his letter was not sugary. He regretted the padding of the three volumes with "indifferent matter." But he did not censure the reactionary spirit in which Margaret had attributed the corruption of an entire village to a course of lectures on secular subjects.

It might be expected that a clever young girl, advised by an older man for whom she felt the greatest reverence, would correct the faults he mentioned. Unfortunately she would always be able to see her failings but never force herself to be rid of them. Throughout her career critics would judge her charitably on the grounds that she had to make money for her dependents. In her heart she knew that this was only an excuse. The Wilsons were not well off, but even in her girlhood, in this her first success, she was in no urgent need. Colburn paid her £150 for *Mrs. Margaret Maitland;* the sum seemed too small to save so she spent it; how, she scarcely knew. Her carelessness about money and her impervious front to criticism were ominous signs for her future. She lacked the fierce ambition of most women writers, nor had she that desire to improve social conditions which had inspired the writer of the new novel *Mary Barton.* Her power of invention was probably greater than that of any other woman novelist of the century; she had it in her to do wonders. But she was impatient and restless, dominated by her mother and ignorant of the world.

A spate of Scottish tales followed, all somber and pious, most of them historical. They were the stories Margaret had heard as a little girl, and were as much her mother's as her own. The young writer seems to have seen every face, and every architectural and natural feature with perfect distinctness of line and color, but it is doubtful if she heard the voices of her characters. Action was lacking, nor was there any hint of the subtle irony which would distinguish her mature writing.

Her life resumed the monotonous course which the months in London had interrupted. The Wilsons moved across the river to Birkenhead; Willie was called to a little church, misbehaved, was fetched home, and sat about the house reading old novels. At last he escaped to Rome, where he pottered about happily for many years. Robert Macpherson employed him profitably in his photographic business, but Willie's best hours were those spent in impressing tourists with his amazing erudition. Margaret did not wish to see him again, but she made over to him the proceeds of several of her novels.

There was one bright interlude in the four years which followed her first London experience. She went with her mother to Edinburgh to visit the family of Dr. Moir, the "Delta" of *Blackwood's Magazine*. Mrs. Wilson was called home, and Margaret was allowed to finish her visit in freedom. Through the kindness of her cousins, the Wilsons, a family of famous scientists, she was introduced to the brilliant literary society of Edinburgh. There she met Major Blackwood, who found her very intelligent and said she expressed the best views on contemporary literature he had ever heard. She had a talk with "Christopher North," a huge, lean lion of an old man who told her kindly that work would not hurt her while she was young and happy. Such meetings were exhilarating and not without practical results, but unluckily Edinburgh celebrities were remembered in such a refulgent light that those she met in London seemed scarcely worth cultivating. She could never find a later love so satisfying as her mother's, never pictures or plays so wonderful as her idea of them, no other society equal to that of Edinburgh in her youth.

"Christopher North" had seen that she was young, but he was

hardly likely to guess that she was not happy. The desire to confess, which lies at the root of most fiction writing, was submerged in her Scottish reticence. No author ever tried harder to keep herself out of her work. She could never pardon writers of memoirs who exposed their family affairs. Perhaps if we had known more of hers than the little at which she hinted, they would strike us as less sinister. She affords us glimpses of an indifferent father, an embittered strong-willed mother, a troublesome Willie, a cheerless home, a young and friendless girl. We expect the lonely little writer to escape her environment, not as did independent Dinah Mulock, who went to London and had her own doorkey, but in the only way open to the Scotch gentlewoman—marriage.

She had been amazed when her cousin Francis Oliphant appeared in Birkenhead to ask her to marry him, and had promptly refused him. When he came again, she accepted. Her mother was not likely to think any suitor good enough for her Margaret, and she disliked Francis, although he was an Oliphant and her near kinsman. When many years later, in 1865, Margaret wrote *Agnes,* she attempted to explain her marriage in such disguise as would baffle the reader but relieve her own mind. Agnes's husband is gay and kind, but he is incapable of the serious view of life which is natural in his young wife. She mortifies him by her social failures; she will not talk, gets herself into a corner, "forgets" to repay calls, and dresses too quietly. He on his part offends her by his levity and his irresponsibility over her widowed future. Nor can she understand how he dares die without anxiety for his soul. The author of *Agnes* seems as puzzled as her heroine by his attitude. A woman may be exceedingly clever in character analysis and yet fail to understand her own husband; and so it seems to have been with Margaret Oliphant.

She married her cousin in Birkenhead May 4, 1852. It was a kind of double wedding, for that morning she received the proofs of *Katie Stewart* (1853) and began the close association with *Blackwood's Edinburgh Magazine* which would continue forty-five years.

Francis loved society and had many friends in London. Unluckily her adoring mother insisted on breaking up the old home and following the young couple. The Wilsons settled so near the Oliphants that daily visits could not be avoided. Mrs. Wilson had the more time for her daughter because her son Frank, jealous of Margaret's love for Francis Oliphant, had married his cousin Jeanie, one of the Edinburgh Wilsons. Young Mr. Oliphant wanted to have his wife admired and looked forward to entertaining in his new home. But Margaret had had no social experience beyond kirk tea-drinkings and a few Edinburgh parties. She could not take her mother when she went out with Francis, and without her she felt shy and self-conscious. She did not approve of her mother's coming to London, yet criticism would have seemed disloyal.

She was distressed when her mother said sharp things to her husband, and angry when he retorted. Had Francis been wealthy, Mrs. Wilson might have been better disposed toward him, but the style of living on which he and Margaret insisted made it necessary for her daughter to write. He worked hard, but had no instinct for business. Nor did his success depend altogether on the beauty and validity of his designs; the windows had to be executed by skilled workmen who were almost invariably unreliable. Margaret liked to write and would have done so in any case, but in Victorian times only a tactful wife could afford to be a breadwinner. Margaret had a sharp Scottish tongue and was inclined to think that Francis took his responsibilities too easily: it is to be supposed that she said much which she regretted afterward.

Katie Stewart, associated with her wedding day, was another of her mother's stories, one which Mrs. Wilson had heard from the withered lips of an aged kinswoman, the "Katie" of the tale. John Blackwood complained that Margaret's version contained altogether too much of her pure Scotch; he suggested shortening the arm and plumping up the shoulder of the patrician lady. Margaret refused to alter "real existencies." Admiration for her courage as an artist diminishes with a knowledge of many subsequent incidents; she would not rewrite, and she was stubborn.

In June, 1853, a daughter was born to the young Oliphants. A year and a day later Margaret gave birth to a second little girl, and grandmother Wilson, who had hitherto been able to conceal her fatal illness, took to her bed. Margaret was torn between her duty to her mother and to the babies at home. Mrs. Wilson suffered greatly and when at last she died, Margaret was horrified at her own extreme relief. Her second child died not long after; she feared this was her punishment for not loving her mother more; it was perhaps because she had loved her too well, for little Marjorie was still a nursing baby. Then a third child was born and died within a day. Margaret very nearly went insane. She moved as in a dream from room to room murmuring Jesus' words, "Yet a little while and ye shall not see Me," and longed in the frantic impetuosity of her heart for the day when she and her little ones should lie still forever.

A son born in late autumn of 1856 aroused her from this dangerous state. He was the fourth child to arrive in a period of three and a half years, during which there had been two little funerals in the house and her mother had died in the next street. Margaret's hopes revived with Cyril and she ceased to look on small Maggie as a blighted flower. The children were exceptionally beautiful and Big Jane was the kindest of young nurses. When she took the little ones for an airing, people stopped her to praise the brown curls and the exquisite Oliphant coloring.

Now Margaret took more pleasure in ordering her house and in society. Her husband's friends, most of them struggling artists, could not afford to give dinners, but were in the agreeable habit of gathering rather late in the evening at one house or another. There the men discussed their work in a studio which had been designed for a drawing room, while their wives chatted and sewed downstairs until it was time to join forces and eat supper.

Although Margaret was continually writing and publishing, her life seemed that of a purely domestic Victorian lady. The evenings she liked best were those passed in her own house without visitors, when her husband was working upstairs in the studio until the light failed, the children were in bed, and she was sewing for them in the downstairs dining room. Now and then she would run up the two flights to the nursery to make sure that little Margaret and the baby were asleep. On her return journey she would step into her bedroom, which was on a corner with street lamps shining in from two sides. The room was tranquil, and a smiling reflection faced her in the dim mirror while she thought with a shock of surprise, that, after all that had happened, she was really a very happy woman.

These few years were her happiest, but outside her home she felt she was nobody. Her husband could not give her the sense of support which her mother had afforded. The young woman, who as a girl had invaded Glasgow homes clamoring for signatures, complained that

she could not possibly talk to strangers at a party. She had talked easily to Edinburgh celebrities, but she suspected that these second-raters
thought her a tongue-tied nonentity. Like Anthony Trollope, Mrs.
Oliphant refused to take herself seriously, but was annoyed when the
rest of the world followed her example. "Grace Greenwood," one of
the band of American women who toured Europe in the 1850's, met
Margaret in the mid-century through hospitable Anna Maria Hall,
and in her travel book passed over her slurringly as "a homely little
Scotchwoman." Mary Howitt was kind to Margaret, not because
she was a novelist, but because she was pregnant. Dinah Mulock's
gaze rested on her with provoking earnestness until Margaret felt
resentfully that her pretty rival was trying to read her mind and found
it wanting.

Very soon family troubles shut her off from this dubious society.
In the spring of 1858, when Cyril was a year and a half old, Francis
Oliphant had a hemorrhage from the lungs. Margaret, always terrified when her children's health was in question, was persuaded that
the occurrence meant nothing, the more easily because she was on
the point of starting with the little ones for an Edinburgh holiday.
But when the headstrong young woman reached her destination, she
became half frantic with anxiety over her husband and spent the
following day, the Sabbath when no trains ran in Scotland, in the
bleak station waiting in vain for a reply to her telegram. Perhaps he
thought she might have worried earlier; at any rate he made her stay
for a letter.

She finished her visit and returned to find him visibly worn and
ostensibly vexed by troubles with his workmen. With Margaret's
approval, he had rented a second smaller house on the same street for
a workshop, in the hope that, when he could supervise the entire

process of construction, he would be more successful. But he was an impractical artist: when a church could afford but one window where a pair was obviously wanted, he donated the second with his wife's sanction. She expressed her contempt for his shoddy artisans and boasted that her maids, who had neither the schooling nor the wages of the men, were loyal and devoted. Francis hated such talk. He could not fail to see how much higher she rated her sex than his. Her earnings were far more than any he could command. If he read *The Quiet Heart* (1854), which ran in *Blackwood's* the year before Mrs. Wilson's death, he must have seen himself in the wretched hero detested by the heroine's mother and in the end roughly reformed.

His doctor sent him to a Harley Street specialist whose house was around the corner from their own. Margaret walked with Francis as far as the door and waited, not without tears, until he rejoined her. There was, he said soothingly, nothing much the matter; rest and a few months in Italy would restore his health. Some two years later, Robert Macpherson told her that Francis had walked out of the doctor's house with the assurance that his case was hopeless. Margaret refused to believe "Mac," because she did not think that Francis would have subjected her to the difficulties of the Italian expedition, had he expected to die and leave his little family stranded. Not only did she feel that the children were more important than their father; she shared the Victorian conviction that her husband ought to protect her, although in her own case she was far better able to protect and cherish him. This is the point of view of *Romola;* again it is what Charlotte Brontë expected of Mr. Nicholls. It is the opinion of many women in the present time.

Francis dismissed his workmen and closed the shop; she broke up her home, sent the furniture into storage, kept only Big Jane to help her with the children. Francis had no money, and she had spent hers as she made it. She arranged with *Blackwood's* to do a series of articles on the Italian scene which would, if accepted, bring in £20 a month.

In a panic over their dearth of resources, the Oliphants traveled in the most frugal and uncomfortable way. The road to Florence was a nightmare of interminable rides in filthy diligences, boats missed, smoky fires in dreary lodginghouses over which Francis sat, silent and shivering. As if to settle in Florence in mid-winter had not been sufficient folly, Margaret engaged an apartment on a dark side street where the sun never penetrated the sitting room in which Francis huddled over the fire and Margaret tried to write. She had become an able critic; her anonymous series on "Modern Novelists" written in her twenties is worth reading today, but the articles she sent from Florence were poor indeed. Sometimes, as if her presence exasperated him, Francis would insist on her going out—to the art galleries—to walk—to gather material—anywhere out of the house. On one sad day she stood long beside the Arno, the tears running down her face while she watched the funeral procession of a princess and heard the remorseless tolling of the bells.

She was pregnant again. There was no living creature to sympathize with her, but she found a confidante in St. Anne in Albertinelli's "Holy Family." It seemed to her that the face held something of her mother's loving look.

There were better days when books arrived from England and Francis listened cheerfully to *The Warden* and argued that *Scenes of Clerical Life* was by the same hand. Occasionally he felt strong enough to visit the Uffizi, but he would return depressed over the contrast between what he had seen and what he himself could accomplish.

At last May came with warmth and sunshine. Margaret, leaning from her window, saw the doorway below heaped high with lilies of the valley; her children ran home from the Boboli gardens with their little hands full of anemones. Now, when the climate might have helped Francis, he insisted on going to Rome. This was not, as Margaret supposed, a caprice; Robert Macpherson lived in Rome and, although Margaret disliked him, his wife Gerardine was her only woman friend; Francis was not indifferent to the fact that, if he died, Margaret would need friends.

The little family spent the early summer with the Macphersons at primitive Nettuno. At first Francis seemed better and even painted a little. Then they moved to Frascati. In *A Son of the Soil* (1866), which Margaret wrote six years later when she was once more "in the depths of despair," she gave a somber account of the lingering death of a young man in that place of sad remembrance. When, on the first of October, the Oliphants moved into Rome, a doctor told them that the sick man was dying. "If that is so, that is no reason why we should be miserable," said Francis tranquilly. Margaret could not understand his words or manner. All the years of her life, the simple statement haunted her. In several of her novels, a dying man repeats it, and she lets slip her wonder at his indifference to "the solemn things that lay before him." Her experience in Catholic countries broadened her views, but she never forgot that much was required of a Scotch Presbyterian.

Six weeks after Francis Oliphant died in Rome, and a fortnight before Christmas 1859, Francis Romano—Cecco, as he was always to be called—was born to a lonely, despairing young woman. As soon as she could travel, she and Big Jane took the children to Birkenhead to the home of her brother Frank. He and his Jeanie were very kind, but Margaret was a woman who loved to give and loathed receiving. She was also of an envious nature, especially where her children were concerned. When Frank's little people ran to meet him at the door, she resented the welcome as if it put a slight on her fatherless little ones. In her defense it should be said that she was not well. One cold followed another and her hair had turned white although she was not yet thirty. She had money troubles, was £800 in debt, and the Blackwoods had regretfully returned several articles and kept some out of kindness but had not been able to publish them. Poor as she was, she took a melancholy pleasure in her extremely becoming mourning, seeing to it that her black dresses were elegant in material and fit.

Mrs. Gaskell had recently described Charlotte Brontë as a woman without hope. Mrs. Oliphant continued to hope in a reckless way, but from this time she was never free from fear. A formless anxiety obsessed her; she had a constant presage of misfortune which would strike at her through her children. The eight years since her marriage had been full of trouble; her own family was completely broken up —her father had disappeared after her mother's death; of her five children two were dead and now she was a widow. In order to support the three precious ones she had salvaged, she must write with an eye to money rather than to fame. Who would care whether or not she became famous? She could indulge in such rational thoughts and even congratulate herself on self-denial; she was, however, choosing the very course which she wanted to pursue. Her extraordinary power of invention, the unquenchable flow of language, the nervous excitement which she strove to conceal, her remembrance of past griefs, all urged her to endless rapid writing. She had also been early infected by her mother's foolish theory of genius and, like almost all contemporary novelists, by the example of the indefatigable Scott.

As soon as she was physically able, she left her brother and settled in Edinburgh, where her literary connections were most promising. In humble mood she engaged the ground-floor apartment in a house in Fetis Row; Big Jane stayed with her and she intended never to part even briefly from the children. But she could not write to any effect, and most of what she submitted was returned. She was utterly discouraged before her will to live pulled her quite suddenly up from the mire. Then she behaved as had Frances Trollope, sick and humiliated in Cincinnati; Elizabeth Gaskell, broken-hearted over her little son's death; Charlotte Brontë, returning from her last sister's grave to solace her grief in *Shirley*. Women writers lift themselves up from the depths; as they rise, each brings with her what she is able to carry.

On the day of resurgence Margaret had forced herself up the hill to ask the Blackwoods to take a serial, and their kindness had shamed her almost more than their refusal. She left the brothers without breaking down, but as she walked home in the rain with the wind flicking her widow's veil against her face, while in the distance a street organ ground out "Charlie is my darling," blank depression descended upon her and she cried and could not stop crying until she reached her own doorstep and must get control of herself or terrify her children. She found them playing, the prettiest little souls, Maggie seven, Cyril three, Cecco only a year, and they struck her as such a delicious contrast to dour Scotch winters and hardhearted publishers that she could do no less than sit down and join the game. She played so madly that the sober Scotchwoman within her said she must be fey. When the small three were tucked into bed, she began the "Carlingford Series."

These novels, which commenced with *The Rector* (1863), itself hardly more than a sketch, and ended more than a decade later with the delightful *Phoebe Junior* (1876), popularized her work and were, if not her best fiction, the genre which suited her talents. Of passion except the maternal she was not capable. She was only thirty-one when, made mentally independent by the deaths of her mother and husband, she commenced to express herself, but she had already borne five children and learned to call sex "the odious question." It was impossible to make a romancist like Charlotte Brontë out of her, and she had not the vein of sentimentality which ran through most of Mrs. Gaskell's work. She would not take herself seriously enough to emulate George Eliot, and, had she had a G. H. Lewes at her elbow, she would have disdained his help. She was hampered in the domestic novel by her disbelief in romantic love and her low opinion of men. In her favor lay her prodigious power of invention, a subtle, subacid humor, a fairly wide experience of life, and a degree of tolerance in religious and social matters gained through her residence in Italy. She had had no schooling, but was a very well read woman. If she could not make a hero, she could provide lovable boys with generous impulses, charming girls, wonderful old women, and cantankerous old men.

The Warden and *Scenes of Clerical Life* suggested the "Carlingford Series" to her fertile mind, but beyond such initiatory hints, her work was independent. She had an amusing advantage over Trollope and George Eliot in her Scotch Presbyterianism, which induced a calm consciousness of her inherent superiority to High, Low, or Broad Churchman, to Dissenter, Roman Catholic, or Freethinker.

As a novelist she could afford to be impartial. As a woman she believed implicitly in the Scriptures and preferred a Roman Catholic to a Latitudinarian.

Trollope liked to have it thought that his knowledge of clerical gentlemen sprang from intuition rather than experience. Mrs. Oliphant said frankly that, though she herself had not been a chapel-goer, she supposed that Methodists and Baptists behaved very much like the Liverpool congregation of Scotch Presbyterians with whom her family had worshiped. An honest, greasy grocer is the chief support of Salem Chapel; the former minister, who has been forcibly retired, lives near the Chapel and is torn between his envy of his young successor and a Christian wish to help him deal with the congregation; the young minister, himself the son of a dissenting preacher, is well-educated, handsome, and debonair. He is appalled at the ignorance of the tradespeople who listen to his preaching and suffers acutely when he visits them in the rooms over their shops, and one and another trots out a pretty daughter with a strong hint that she would be a good minister's wife.

Mrs. Oliphant had a very good understanding of the problems of a youthful dissenting minister; he was usually the son of a rural minister and had almost certainly been the cleverest boy in his father's charge. In such youths the habit of speculation was inbred. Oxford and Cambridge were closed to the young man, but there were other universities where he could receive an excellent education. In a social sense he was bound to suffer. His congregation would be his inferiors in manners, culture, and education. Adherents of the Church of England would not ask him to dinner. The Unitarians, whose mental level was far above that of the Episcopalians, were equally inaccessible because in the opinion of Methodists and Baptists they were worse than unprivileged heathen. A high-spirited young man was also certain to resent the power of the congregation; the Baptists acknowledged no overlord but God, and in their earthly puissance called and disposed of a minister as it suited them.

One of Mrs. Oliphant's young men had become a Dissenter from conscientious reasons, but finding conditions intolerable, and being possessed of private means, he deserted to the Establishment. Some of her ministers were thick-skinned; the glowing Phoebe, disdained by the hero of *Salem Chapel,* marries his successor, whose grammar is poor but whose language is unctuous and manner hearty. He becomes pastor of a wealthy London congregation, but he never becomes a gentleman. His daughter, the charming heroine of *Phoebe Junior* (1876), has an excellent education, is very pretty and far superior mentally to the young "ladies" of Carlingford. But Mrs. Oliphant will not allow her to marry the young clergyman who loves her; instead she bestows her on an elephantine boor, son of a millionaire bully who supports her father's London chapel: Mrs. Oliphant had an inflexible sense of caste.

George Eliot had commented on Mrs. Gaskell's unfortunate "love of sharp contrasts." She could have said the same of Margaret Oliphant, who had early begun to introduce into each novel a bizarre incident, a fantastic character, a situation beyond the scope of the domestic. On the surface this appeared due to a feeling that the public must have a sop of melodrama, but when the eccentricity appears in upwards of one hundred novels, we suspect that it is the visible sign of her own hunger for excitement. She was, as Barrie shrewdly observed, something of a Bohemian. Her sternly repressed appetites showed even more plainly in her attitude toward money, which she spent the more recklessly because she was always tortured by a fear of ruin. She confessed to a pleasure found in the taking of a risk. Physically too she was restless. Although she loved her home and spent time and thought in filling it with rare and beautiful objects, she continued to take long and exhausting journeys even after infirmities made walking an impossibility. During her years in Windsor her frantic haste to catch the afternoon train from London was due almost as much to the necessity of constant movement as to any simple desire for home.

As soon as the "Carlingford Series" was well begun she settled in London, giving as her reason for the move the convenience of being near another publisher, Mr. Blackett of Hurst and Blackett. His wife had been friendly to her, and he had offered himself as an escort from Italy after her husband's death. London possessed another attraction in the Carlyles, with whom she had become acquainted while preparing her life of Edward Irving, the famous preacher and founder of the Apostolic church, who in youth had been tutor to Jane Carlyle. The old, childless couple became much attached to the young, widowed Margaret Oliphant.

Her life of Irving (1862) was followed at long intervals by four biographies of contemporaries, preachers, or men such as Count de Montalembert (1872) and Lawrence Oliphant (1891) who were deeply interested in spiritual problems. She enjoyed writing biography far more than novels; she knew how to build up a character, had a great respect for facts, and was a competent though not profound research worker. Like most Victorians she felt that it was right to suppress much which would have led to a better understanding of a subject. She labored under unusual disadvantages, such as her intimacy with Principal Tulloch's wife and Alice Oliphant, and the distressing helpfulness of the Montalembert ladies. Today no one would care to read these books, but her tenderly whimsical *St. Francis of Assisi* and her delightful sketches of the reign of Queen Anne and of the second George have retained a literary value.

Several busy and successful years were spent in Ealing, during which she appeased her restlessness by keeping her house full of guests. Gerardine Macpherson came from Rome in 1864 and was nursed through a long summer's illness. When she was able to go back, she begged Margaret to come with her. As it happened, Principal Tulloch, the eminent Scottish divine, had been ordered away on a Mediterranean voyage and in his absence Mrs. Tulloch agreed to accompany Gerardine and Margaret. The three adventurous Victorian ladies with their children and nurses started off in wonderfully good spirits, rejoicing in freedom from male supervision, but far too well-bred to talk about it. Margaret, as the leading spirit, insisted on their traveling comfortably.

Arrived in Rome, they took a house and settled themselves to enjoy the winter. Margaret was not depressed by the memories of her husband's death in the city; he had been dead for five years. Then a catastrophe occurred; her oldest child, twelve-year-old Maggie, who had been her greatest comfort, a little mother to the boys, took Roman fever, died and was buried beside her father. It is no exaggeration to say that Margaret's heart broke. She separated from her friends and wandered over western Europe, her remaining children clutched to her breast. She took with her their nurse and a governess, because she could not endure the thought of depriving them of any advantage, and settled now in a sunny apartment on the Champs Elysées, now in a house of Queen Christina at St. Adresse. For the first few months she kept the two little Tulloch girls with her, feeling that if she parted from them she would never be able to endure seeing them again. At night in her exhaustion she slept briefly and woke before dawn to her familiar desolation.

Yet she wrote continually, saw a great deal that was interesting, and met a number of striking personalities from suave and stately Count de Montalembert, whose life she would write for the Blackwoods a few years later, to shabby Father Prout, who sang her his own "Bells of Shandon" looking, she thought, like a fine ivory carving. The American actress, Charlotte Cushman, whom she had ridiculed in London for her hoarse declamation of the "Sands o' Dee," was wonderfully kind to her in Paris. In short, Mrs. Oliphant had reason to rate her experiences of society as far greater than Charlotte Brontë's or those of George Eliot in George Lewes's hothouse, but these experiences were too complex for her to handle without reflection; she could not get their full value without giving herself time, and this she would not do. Besides, she had determined never to look too deep into human problems or, if she must look, never to reveal all she found there.

After eighteen months of aimless wandering, her feeling of responsibility toward her boys forced her to return to England. In her despair she had thought of settling in a primitive Italian town and letting them grow up there healthy and untaught; when she regained mental stability, she determined to educate them as English scholars and gentlemen, sending them through Eton and Oxford, an expensive course which her Victorian friends blamed as an example of doting mother love. It is difficult to see what else she could have done. Whatever talents the boys possessed were those of potential scholars. They had not the physical hardihood for business careers, and there was no one from whom they would inherit money or estates.

Mrs. Oliphant's worse mistake was natural enough in a self-made woman; having had no schooling herself, she regarded the "serious" or "precious" student with cynical amusement; as a result Cyril and Cecco would have thought shame to be found among the "grinds." She was certainly too much the man of the family, the "good provider" of Victorian days, and spared the boys all anxiety as to means.

Financially she was already doing very well. Even a small annuity is a great comfort to a widow with children, and Queen Victoria had granted her a pension of £100 a year. The Blackwoods paid her £1500 for *The Perpetual Curate* (1864), the same sum Smith and Elder paid Charlotte Brontë, not for one novel but for the combined three. The brothers Blackwood had a high opinion of Mrs. Oliphant's ability, and urged upon her the duty of becoming one of the first rank of British novelists.

To her relief—for she did not really wish to reform—an accident of life made it appear right and even generous to continue her headlong production. Her brother Frank went bankrupt and was unable to educate his only son, another Frank Wilson, three years older than her Cyril. Mrs. Oliphant took him into her house, sent him to Eton with her own boys and later to Cooper's Hill, where he prepared for the Indian Civil Service. A good and gifted young fellow, he gave her reason to be proud of him. She wrote John Blackwood that the bringing up of three fine men who would do honorable work in the world was a sufficient apology for her literary shortcomings.

Then her brother's wife Jeanie died in Hungary, where the luckless Frank had settled his family. Margaret was horrified to learn that her incapacitated brother was coming with his two little girls to live with her in Windsor. A Scottish gentlewoman could not refuse a home to her kinsfolk; Mrs. Oliphant moved into a larger house and met, not without difficulty, her greatly increased expenses. Frank was obviously unfit to earn his own living. He distressed her by haunting the dining room where she did her writing. The brother and sister who had once loved each other now agreed upon nothing. His little girls did not interest her. They were quiet, small creatures, not much in the way, not costing much, but annoying fixtures. A cousin had come on a visit and, as she had no home, remained and took much of the housekeeping on herself. Numerous servants had to be paid: money simply flowed away in that establishment. Margaret herself liked pretty clothes, collected lace and *objets d'art*. She could not endure absence from her sons and was unable to make suitable literary friendships in London because she preferred to rush through her business and take an afternoon train home to her boys. When she stayed in town, she had them with her so that she could take them to the theatre. In Windsor, she would go to Evensong at the College and bring a group of their friends home to supper. Yet she did not overestimate the talents, the charm and beauty of her sons.

At moments when her burden seemed more than she could bear, she told herself that the year 1875 would mark her liberation. Cyril would then enter Oxford, young Frank would sail for India, and the little girls go to school in Germany. On the eve of these changes, her worst charge, her brother Frank, died rather suddenly; in the future she would have only Cecco at home with her.

In the summer of 1875, she celebrated her release by taking the three boys to Switzerland; she wished especially to do something handsome for young Frank, who was to start for India in the autumn. During this vacation she made friends of Anne Thackeray and her sister, the first Mrs. Leslie Stephen, and of Stephen himself, at that time editor of the *Cornhill*. He took two of her long novels for serial publication, paying her a sum sufficient to cover her expenses for the next two years. Her new freedom from family cares, the generous payment, and her association with these charming people who belonged in the highest literary circle suggested that here was an opportunity, perhaps the last she would have, for doing really admirable work. A request from Alexander Macmillan added persuasion: T. A. Trollope's history of Florence had been a great disappointment to him and he believed that Mrs. Oliphant could write exactly the kind of book he wanted.

Margaret Oliphant was fifty-three when these opportunities presented themselves. Had she been an ambitious woman, had she been less absorbed in her sons, less inhibited, she might yet have become the outstanding woman writer of the century. Undoubtedly she made greater efforts in the colorful, charming *Makers of Florence* (1876) and in the books on Venice, Rome, and Edinburgh which followed at long intervals over twenty years. They were written after careful but not exhaustive study; she could not now join the company of scholars, whom she called "darkling moles." So much has been learned, so much has been well written, since her day that these works have been superseded. Yet they retain the quality of life; to read them is to feel interest quickened, to be urged to go further, which is perhaps the best recommendation to be given the historical works of the nineteenth century. The novel is longer lived, and if Mrs. Oliphant had devoted two years instead of six months to *A Country Gentleman and His Family*, we should not now be sighing over the oblivion of her fame.

For the next fifteen years she had an aristocratic public. The historian Kinglake dreaded the moment when he would finish reading

It Was a Lover and His Lass (1883) until he knew that *The Ladies Lindores* (1883) was ready for the press. She was told that she was Darwin's favorite author, and with her usual impolitic shrugging off of compliments, said that was because he liked happy endings. John Blackwood engaged her as editor of "Foreign Classics for English Readers," to which she contributed *Dante* (1877) and *Cervantes* (1880), and her son Cyril, *De Musset*. Her *Century of Great Poets* made good reading. Her critical articles on contemporary and historical French works were admirable; as a reviewer she never trusted a translation of French or Italian writers. Russian she could not read, but her article on Turgenev written in 1886 shows remarkable comprehension of the provincial scene.

Yet she could hardly take pleasure in her successes as a writer because every advance in her profession was matched by a fresh womanly grief. Young Frank died in India. Cyril, whose record at Eton promised a brilliant career at Oxford, got into a fast set, exhausted his health and her means, and although not a failure as a student, fell far below what she had a right to expect. He came home and for a time read for the bar, going up to London daily. Perhaps he was already ill, perhaps his mother's anxious surveillance had given a weak nature no opportunity to develop strength; whatever the reason, Cyril had no ambition, no hope. He sat about the house much as Uncle Willie had done long ago in Liverpool, as his Uncle Frank had done in his own boyhood. His mother had a third, more poignant memory of her son's father shivering and silent, crouched over a fire in a chill Italian room. A secretary's post was found for Cyril in Ceylon, but the climate routed him and he returned almost immediately. He had literary talents but no vigor, and died in 1890 at the age of thirty-four.

Mr. and Mrs. Oliphant had been cousins and Cecco had been

born after the death of his tubercular father. He was a delicate young fellow, but a delightful one, and was deeply attached to his mother. His tastes were scholarly, his habits industrious, and with health he would probably have accomplished all that she could have asked as her own apology for faulty work. They were always together; he collaborated with her in the still read volumes on English literature and published several articles in *Blackwood's*. He died of tuberculosis complicated by heart trouble in 1894. Out of her family only the once unwanted nieces were left to her. They were grateful, loving, and good; she had many friends and a charming house, but house and heart were desolate.

In 1880, in her first anxiety as to Cyril's behavior, she had begun a series of tales about the unseen world. Mrs. Oliphant could tell a good ghost story, but could not believe in one; these were spiritual rather than spiritualistic and centered for the most part upon the adventures of a Little Pilgrim in the life after death. A gentle, not overly intelligent neighbor had provided the model—a certain Nelly who had taken care of an invalid mother and brother; the good creature had lived as long as she was needed and then died unobtrusively in her sleep, leaving Mrs. Oliphant to imagine her adventures in the spiritual world. After the death of Cyril, these stories became intensely personal: unable to regard the future of her dead boy in the light of Calvinism, she invented a Land of Suspense where he could learn the lessons he had scorned on earth. These tales meant a great deal to the literal of her generation and it is probable that many of today's bereaved would find comfort in them. In a literary sense, the two which are least personal are the best: *A Beleaguered City* (1880), which has recently been republished, and the delightful "Old Lady Mary"; both of which should film well. Mrs. Oliphant's short ghost story, "The Open Door," is still a favorite with collectors.

Three years after Cecco's death, the publisher J. M. Dent came to Windsor to beg her for a book on Siena. He had a great admiration for the works of "that wonderful woman" and the sight of the frail, exquisite old lady against a background of rare and beautiful things gave him a lively aesthetic pleasure. She said she would write the book for him but must first revisit Siena. Ill and old as she seemed, he believed she could do it; her dark, undimmed eyes spoke an indomitable will; she was not a woman to die before she was ready.

He did not know how more than ready she was; she longed to follow her children. She went to Siena, but she did not write his book. Nor could she finish the *History of the House of Blackwood*, of which two volumes are by her hand; and yet perhaps no other author left so little unpublished work.

In the 'nineties she often complained that she was out of fashion. The Victorians were dying out; the Carlyles, whom she had loved; Trollope and Reade, whom she had admired, her enemies, Froude and Ruskin (who did not know they were her enemies—but they had attacked those she admired); George Eliot, whom she had envied, all were gone. Tennyson too was dead; she had gone to his funeral in Westminster Abbey with Anne Thackeray and Ellen Terry. In the place of the old Victorian woman novelist there had arisen a new species: Mrs. Humphrey Ward, who tore the Bible to pieces, and Sarah Grand, who wrote about sex.

Mrs. Oliphant, who had been born into a Liberal family, had not advanced with the century. Perhaps the domestic novelist has to be a reactionary, because success depends on the creation of a world unaffected by ulterior changes. In Mrs. Oliphant's later criticism, a pettish note, a grandmotherly voice denounced new ways. "Oh! if the Queen had been but always young; if our Sovereign Lady had been always happy, always at the head of her own Court, always exercising that wise Control in Society as in other regions!" Mrs. Oliphant's detestation of sex had deepened; with cold finality she advised women to think more of their clothes than of their bodies because fashions "have their moral uses." "What a happy thing it is that Christianity knows no 'Sex-question'!" she exclaimed, recklessly voicing the misconception of many Victorian ladies.

In the 'nineties it was often said, "Mrs. Oliphant is to the English world of letters what Victoria is to England." There was an almost comical resemblance between the widows of Windsor; both had become ideal Victorian ladies. They were notable among the honorable women who were "widows indeed," bereaved mothers, staunch supporters of the Home and the Christian faith, patient bearers of uncommon burdens. Margaret Oliphant had not "bowed the knee to Baal" in the matter of modern scientific trends; she believed the Bible, and knew that God was her Father and Jesus her Elder Brother. But if the century had not repressed Margaret, she may be said to have repressed her century.

Victoria's Jubilee was set for June 22, 1897. Mrs. Oliphant, who had once had no very great admiration for the sovereign lady and had even poked fun at her literary production, had long ago accepted her as the symbol of what was best for Britons. The Queen had shown her personal kindness, writing to her at her son's death, receiving her at Windsor and visiting her at the little house. Mrs. Oliphant's article " 'Tis Sixty Years Since" in *Blackwood's* May number (1897) honored the long reign in admirable style.

Before it was published, her doctor had told her she was dying, a piece of news which she accepted with pleasure. But she did not wish to spoil the coming festivities for her household and, by an act of will, stretched her life out to the twenty-fifth of June, three days after the Jubilee. She did not seem to suffer. In her extreme weakness, she submitted to being carried from her bed to a couch by the window; unable to hold a book, she asked to be read Tennyson's "Crossing the Bar" and Lockhart's account of the death of her old hero, Scott. She was perfectly sure that she was going to her children, and at the last said tranquilly, "I seem to see nothing but God and my Lord."

Thus died a very tired old woman who had had a sad life. Whether or not her misfortunes could have been avoided is not our question; our chief concern is that one who wrote so well should have written no better. When the tablet to her memory was unveiled in St. Giles, which she had made the more memorable in *Royal Edinburgh* (1890), Barrie paid her one of the handsomest tributes a Victorian gentleman could pay a Victorian lady: Mrs. Oliphant was, he said, greater as a woman than as a writer. In modern ears, the compliment has a dubious ring. The griefs which the world knew made her, not great, but greatly to be pitied.

Perhaps her worst suffering came from her private conviction of failure. In her frequently begun, hastily broken off, and wholly unsatisfactory *Autobiography* (1899), she reveals a profound dissatisfaction with the quality of her work. She repeats the excuse that the circumstances of her life forced her to overproduction and careless writing, but adds candidly that she might have made almost as much money by cutting the volume of her work in half. Her characters, she complains, do not interest her; not one of her heroines is as real to her as Scott's Jeanie Deans. She had never given herself time to become acquainted with them. Her cynical disbelief in the existence of the heroic, her feeling that men were at the best but poor creatures, her positive aversion to any passion except the maternal, were other hindrances to the novelist.

But should any reader be tempted to take up a novel by Margaret Oliphant written in the 1860's or later, he is not unlikely to find himself settling contentedly to a long winter's reading. *The Curate in Charge* is perhaps the most perfect, *Miss Majoribanks* and *Phoebe Junior* are very diverting, *The Sorceress* presents an excellent picture of Victorian upper-middle-class manners and morals; I confess my own preference for the cheerfully cynical *Greatest Heiress in England*. Only a few of the enormous number of novels fall below or rise above these five. Mrs. Oliphant's reputation has been smothered by the weight of her volumes, not one of which could satisfy her own fastidious taste.

*Oh never star
Was lost here but it rose afar*

ROBERT BROWNING

Homekeeping Hearts

THE WOMEN with whom we have been consorting represent a group without precedent or parallel in literary history. In order to estimate their ultimate significance, let us gather together the principal points of our discoveries and reassess the domestic soil from which all alike derived their spiritual nourishment.

Beneath the acquired habits which dominated life and literary labor lay the fundamental training which these novelists received as children. Though subjected to a discipline which, by modern standards, would be judged repressive, there is no reason to believe that any one of them was abused in a physical or psychic sense. Mrs. Wood, the silliest of our ladies, and Mrs. Oliphant, the least sentimental, were family pets; Harriet Martineau and Eliza Lynn Linton retained a strong resentment because, owing to the size and formidable composition of their families, they had not been able to dominate their households; Charlotte Brontë from the age of nine directed the private affairs of her sisters and brother.

The schooling of all these writers was meager; each was really self-educated. Out of individual observation and discrimination, from reading, travel, and society, there gradually developed a number of finely individualized women whose literary skill originated a group of highly finished characters. Those minor authors, who were ignorant of the existence of art canons, wrote with a happy spontaneity. But all were women of uncommon intelligence, capable of understanding philosophical concepts, and yet so subservient to religious dogma and to masculine domination that very few of them ventured into realms of abstract thought. Most of them supposed there was nothing left on which to speculate because God, the Church, and the Gentlemen had solved all higher problems. The intellectual and social significance of the bulk of their novels is negligible because the society they helped to consolidate was based on principles already established.

These women, all of whom came from homes which although faulty were in every case respectable, displayed in their own maturity a domesticity little short of passionate. The way women live ordains the way they work; their domestic manners are an indication of taste and of tact, determinants of subject and treatment. An appraisal of the customs of a period so remote as that of the Victorians requires unusual discretion; we must not confuse taste with fashion or suppose that those ladies whose standards most resemble our own were therefore less parochial.

We know nothing of Mrs. Crowe's home life and very little of Mrs. Clive's, although, if Miss Mitford was correct in her assertion that Mr. Clive's income was £20,000 a year, the family housekeeping was probably relegated to a competent staff. Of Mrs. Norton at home we have scarcely a glimpse beyond the sight of her brilliant beauty half hidden by the ruffled curtains of the little balconied drawingroom on Birdcage Walk where she sat waiting to receive Lord Melbourne's visits. Mrs. Gore, perfectly dressed, her face clear-cut as disks of ivory upon an Indian screen, went much into society, where she never spoke to a woman when a man was within reach.

Despite the evidence of her ten children, Mrs. Gore does not strike us as a home body; but no stranger may pry into the heavy years of blindness and seclusion.

Mary Howitt was exceedingly hospitable but had too many children and too little money to carry out elaborate schemes of household decoration—she wrote and published in a welter of care. Mrs. Craik and Mrs. Gaskell, who were prosperous authors, bought fine houses with their earnings. Mrs. Hall entertained liberally, both in the Rosery and in her country house, and was especially cordial to visitors from America. Her husband was one of those unfortunate people who utter pure truth so that it sounds like a lie; but where he was a hindrance, her ancient mother was a social asset, singing and playing charmingly and conversing in purest French with guests from the Continent. Harriet Martineau used to rise at seven and make her own coffee before she seated herself at the task of enlightening the British nation. She too built a house which she loved like a child. Had Eliza Lynn Linton been a less meticulous housekeeper, her husband might not have left her to seek liberty in America.

Mrs. Oliphant collected laces, copied Jane Carlyle's famous picture screen, covering her replica with tiny French prints. She despised Regency furniture, shuddered at William IV, and filled her drawing room with slender-legged Queen Anne tables and chairs. When one came to tea at Mrs. Oliphant's, not milk but rich cream was poured from the jug, and the food, unlike small beer, was worthy to be chronicled. All these novelists employed servants for the rough work of the house, but they knew how it should be performed and frequently lent a hand to it. Mary Mitford, whom we have arbitrarily excluded from our galaxy, with the assistance of her small household carpeted every room, made chintz covers for the parlor furniture, curtains—including blinds—for the windows all over the cottage, and triumphantly finished her renovations with a dimity-hung four-poster bed.

This almost universal "house-proud" attitude was reflected in these women's novels: an air of daintiness and yet of vigor blows along the descriptive page; the Victorian house even without husband or children has become a symbol of the ideal English way of life. Significantly, Mrs. Oliphant's pleasantest houses are those in which a widow lives with her grown children.

It may seem odd that these homemaking women were not home-keeping. On the contrary, they were restless, requiring frequent changes of scene. Those in meager circumstances managed a run up to London to see the play and talk with the publisher; the fortunate set off for the Continent. No one ever lacked a good excuse for travel: health, culture, material—all were to be found in any place but home. Charlotte Brontë, imbedded as she was in Haworth, made many attempts to change her environment; George Eliot was plagued by an ailment which was alleviated by the treatments at the German baths; Mrs. Gaskell fled before reviews; Mrs. Howitt and Mrs. Hall pursued local color. The effect of travel on the novels of our friends was not wholly beneficial, partly because most of them moved in coveys and saw more of each other than of the foreign scene; the pages of description might have been collected more efficiently from a guidebook. Indeed, the English woman novelist never seemed at home in Europe. Miss Edwards's intellect was able to grasp the abstract meaning of the Risorgimento, but she could not create an Italian revolutionary; George Eliot knew all about Florence, but could conceive of Romola only as an English woman.

Elizabeth Gaskell, that redoubtable housekeeper and reproach to all slatterns, did not admit, and perhaps never knew, that the very perfection of Plymouth Grove made her ill; in her opinion it was the unwholesome air of Manchester. Her habit of staying contentedly for weeks at a time in the Parisian apartment of the incorrigibly untidy Madame Mohl suggests her relief at an escape from her own machinery. In brief, for most novelists the home was a sacred fane worthy of all kinds of immolation except that of constant attendance. Travel was fundamentally an escape.

The presence of a gentleman in the home sometimes drove the woman novelist out of it. For it must not be supposed that our friends, who followed the lead of men in religion and philosophy, approved the behavior of the average male in more mundane matters. Throughout the first half of the century, but especially since good Queen Adelaide had begun to exert a salutary influence on society, the ladies of the upper middle class had been struggling with the problem of uplifting the British Home. They insisted that their men folk should behave decently within its portals so that their children could grow up in a pure atmosphere. Too soon a son must go out into the world's temptations, but a daughter ought to be spared a knowledge of evil until she was old enough to cope with it. In this intention lay two reasons for meticulous housekeeping: theoretically it made home attractive to the husband and safe for the family.

Married women believed that the preservation of the home was worth what it cost them as individuals to submit to the laws of God. His statutes did not require them to be tolerant of "drunkenness, wantonness and chambering" within the precincts of home, nor did He expect them to allow smoking in the drawing room. He had, however, from earliest times, and again by the mouth of Saint Paul, ordered wives to submit themselves to their husbands in the marital relation. This involved the patient endurance of repeated confinements, frequently interspersed with miscarriages, and the painful anxiety lest children be left motherless—with the assurance that this depressing state of affairs would continue until the husband died or one grew too old to bear children. Clergymen and many physicians disapproved the use of chloroform in childbirth, while husbands and wives hesitated to break the Old Testament tabu which had specifically stated that women should bring forth in sorrow. Besides the unavoidable ill-health which often resulted from these frequent pregnancies, sensitive women innocently sought excuse from what they conceded was a duty in neuroses, especially in anxiety headaches, and in escape through long visits and European travel.

Women who wrote books were neither more nor less prolific than the inarticulate: Mrs. Trollope bore seven children, Mrs. Gore ten; Mrs. Oliphant was confined five times in eight years; Elizabeth Browning, marrying after forty, had one normal birth and four miscarriages. Naturally, married writers took a less romantic view of the sexual relation than that held by spinsters, who, dealing with passion from intuition and imagination, often arrived more nearly than the harassed matron at the wonder and beauty of completion. To the married novelist the subject was usually what Mrs. Oliphant called it, "the odious question of sex." But to ignore or deny is not to annul. Avoidance of the central problem of their lives limited the depth of their work, at the same time promoting its diffusion. Their novels never attained the supreme height of excellence, although, as in *Villette* and in *Middlemarch,* the novelist came in sight of Pisgah. The achievement of the group was the permeation of bourgeois society with a consciousness of the novel as a respectable representation of life on the level plane of existence.

While the connection between experience and creation in the Victorian age defies exact formulation, something of the workings of that relation may be apprehended in the lives of the four major women novelists whose histories we possess. Elizabeth Gaskell, who made an early and comparatively happy marriage, and lived the usual life of a well-bred Victorian woman in fortunate circumstances, used as source material only the easily traced memories of her childhood, tales of the countryside, and events and characters which came under her conscious observation. Margaret Oliphant, who was early widowed and repressed her natural instincts through the entire period of her original creative work, withheld herself not only from revealing her own private life, but even from knowing her characters with the intimacy of which she was easily capable. Thus her novels are objective comedies of manners on which she looks with tired, ironic eyes. George Eliot and Charlotte Brontë, whose strong sexual instincts were thwarted, drew from the depths of the unconscious, and fused the images and impressions of their private and recondite worlds with their acquired materials. Contemporary readers, catching glimpses of fascinating but forbidden torments and delights, accepted with docility and relief the assurance that the loves of the Brontë novels were spiritual; of George Eliot's, intellectual.

When criticism has said its arbitrary say, these women still assert a permanent claim on our sympathy and interest, because each is a memorable figure in the universal pattern of striving, satisfaction, failure, and creation. They, and the characters in their novels, are detached, highly finished pieces of an identical human texture. With passing years, the writer has merged into her creations; and truth may be found less in records of these dead women than in the novels they have left us.

Bibliographical Notes

I TAKE GREAT PLEASURE in expressing my thanks to the John Simon Guggenheim Memorial Foundation for the fellowship under which this book was written; to the Librarians of Widener and Houghton Libraries, Harvard University; to Mrs. Flora Livingston of the Harry Elkins Widener Memorial Library, Harvard University; to my son, Richard Poate Stebbins and to Professor Jacques Barzun, who very kindly read the manuscript and suggested numerous changes. Responsibility for the content of the book is mine alone.

The following references are to sources of information *about* the women in this book. They have been useful to me and may be so to the student. But the novels written *by* the women have been the fountains from which I have drawn deepest and if there is anything of value in the foregoing pages it has come from them.

GENERAL WORKS

G. M. Young's *Victorian England* (London, 1936) provides an authoritative background and lists the most important publications by years. Esmé Wingfield-Stratford's *The Victorian Tragedy* (London, 1930) and *Those Earnest Victorians* (New York, 1930) are readable books by a late Victorian with a poor opinion of girls in the 1930's. E. E. Kellett's *Religion and Life in the Early Victorian Age* (London [1938]) is a pleasant, painstaking little book which has been useful in several connections. *Women Novelists of Queen Victoria's Reign* (London, 1897), a symposium in honor of the Jubilee, reflects nineteenth-century opinions. Margaret Oliphant's " 'Tis Sixty Years Since" in *Blackwood's,* May, 1897, is a brief résumé of the reign as it appeared to an accomplished Victorian. J. A. Froude's *Letters and Memorials of Jane Welsh Carlyle* (London, 1883) and Alexander Carlyle's *New Letters and Memorials of Jane Welsh Carlyle* (London, 1903), A. G. K. L'Estrange's *The Friendships of Mary Russell Mitford* (London, 1882), Henry F. Chorley's *The Letters of Mary Russell Mitford*, 2nd Series (London, 1872), *The Diary, Reminiscences and Correspondence of Henry Crabb Robinson* (London, 1869), as well as many other memoirs and diaries of the period, contain interesting allusions to these novelists.

ELIZA LYNN LINTON, 1822–1898

(*Phillips Biographical Reference Index* [1881], p. 609, gives birth incorrectly as in 1828. *Universal Pronouncing Dictionary of Biography and Mythology* [1915], p. 1159, gives b. Keswick, 1822, m. 1858.)

George Somes Layard's *Mrs. Lynn Linton; Her Life, Letters, and Opinions* (London, 1901) is especially valuable as commentary on Mrs. Linton's *Autobiography of Christopher Kirkland* (London, 1885). Her own *My Literary Life* (London, 1899), with an informative introduction by Beatrice Harraden, contains Mrs. Lynn Linton's memories of Dickens, Thackeray, and George Eliot. H. C. Minchin's *Walter Savage Landor: Last Days, Letters and Conversations* (London [1934]) gives some account of her friendship with Landor, and Gordon Haight's *George Eliot and John Chapman* (New Haven, 1940) mentions her difficulties with *Realities*. Hints of her gentler age are to be found in the Diary of Shirley Brooks (1864; unpublished, Houghton Library) and in Jane Ellen Panton's *Leaves from a Life* (London, 1908). W. J. Linton's *Autobiographical Memories* (London, 1895) contains references to Mrs. Howitt (p. 48), Mrs. Craik (p. 171), Mrs. Hall (pp. 66–74), but with almost unparalleled gallantry makes no mention of his own wife, Eliza Lynn Linton. Helen C. Black in *Notable Women Authors of the Day* (Glasgow, 1893), devotes a chapter to Mrs. Lynn Linton. The book is a reprint of interviews illustrated by terrifying photographs and is interesting because it describes the cluttered furnishings of lady authors' houses and the costumes in which they received. Mrs. Linton had designed and embroidered her chair seats, cushions, and fire screen; but we note with relief that "the big green frog and the swallows hanging on the left" were not the work of her hands. Robert Esmonde Sencourt in *The Life of George Meredith* (New York, 1929), p. 158, quotes Meredith's reason for rejecting Mrs. Linton's works.

MRS. CLIVE (CAROLINE MEYSEY-WIGLEY), 1801–1873

Dictionary of National Biography (IV, 559–560)

Adeline Sergeant wrote the chapter "Mrs. Archer Clive" in *Women Novelists of Queen Victoria's Reign* (London, 1897). Eric Partridge furnished a biographical introduction to the edition of *Paul Ferroll* (London, 1928). Henry F. Chorley's *The Letters of Mary Russell Mitford* (London, 1872), *The Diary, Reminiscences, and Correspondence of Henry Crabb Robinson* (London, 1869), and the letters of Elizabeth Barrett Browning contain other references.

HARRIET MARTINEAU, 1802–1876

Harriet Martineau's Autobiography, edited by M. J. Chapman (London, 1877), is a vigorous, cheerful, self-conceited book. Theodora Bosanquet's *Harriet Martineau; an Essay in Comprehension* (London, 1927) is humorous, delightful, and sound. John Cranstoun Nevill's *Harriet Martineau* (London, 1943) is sound but not delightful. Margaret Oliphant wrote a devastating review of the *Autobiography* for *Blackwood's,* April, 1877. Thomas Carlyle's *Reminiscences,* edited by J. A. Froude (London, 1881), pp. 439–440, and the various collections of Mrs. Carlyle's letters contain references to the Carlyles' friendship with Miss Martineau. Una Pope-Hennessey includes Miss Martineau in her *Three English Women in America* (London, 1929). The introduction to Gerardine Bate Macpherson's *Memoir of the Life of Anna Jameson* (Paris, 1878) expresses the resentment against Miss Martineau which was felt by many contemporaries. It was impossible for Victorians to ignore Miss Martineau, and such references to her may be found in most of the diaries and letters of the time, as in Janet Ross, *The Fourth Generation* (New York, 1912), p. 244.

MRS. CROWE (CATHERINE STEVENS), 1800–1876

Webster's *Biographical Dictionary* (1943), p. 371; *Dictionary of National Biography* (V, 237); Sir John A. Hammerton's *Concise Universal Biography* (II, 464)

Adeline Sergeant wrote on her in *Women Novelists of Queen Victoria's Reign*. A. B. Harlan and J. Lee Harlan, Jr., *Letters from Owen Meredith to Robert and Elizabeth Barrett Browning* (Baylor University, Texas, 1937; pp. 69–70) refers to Mrs. Crowe's arrest. Anne Thackeray Ritchie in *Chapters from Some Memoirs* (London, 1894) describes the party for Charlotte Brontë. Harriet Martineau in her *Autobiography* (I, 435) refers to her friendship with Mrs. Crowe. The quotation from Mrs. Carlyle is in Leonard Huxley's *Jane Welsh Carlyle: Letters to Her Family (1839–1863)* (London, 1924), p. 200.

THE HON. MRS. NORTON (CAROLINE SHERIDAN), 1808–1877

Dictionary of National Biography (XIV, 651–653); Hammerton's *Concise Universal Biography* (III, 1046)

Jane Gray Perkins is the author of an excellent biography, *The Life of Mrs. Norton* (London, 1909). Copies of Mrs. Norton's pamphlets, *A Plain Letter to the Lord Chancellor on The Infant Custody Bill,* 1839, and *English Laws for Women in the Nineteenth Century* (privately printed, London, 1854), are in the Boston Public Library. Houghton Library, Harvard University, contains Bertha Coolidge's *Some Unrecorded Letters of Caroline Norton* ([Boston] 1934). Annie Hector Alexander wrote the chapter on Mrs. Norton in *Women Novelists of Queen Victoria's Reign* (London, 1897). S. M. Ellis in *George Meredith; His Life and Friends in Relation to His Work* (London, 1919) and R. E. Sencourt in *The Life of George Meredith* (London, 1929) touch on the origin of Diana. The letters of Frederick Tennyson in the chapter by Charles Tennyson, in *Tennyson and His Friends,* ed. by Hallam, Lord Tennyson (London, 1911), p. 41, and Hester Thackeray Ritchie's *Thackeray and His Daughter* (New York and London, 1924) contain amusing allusions to Mrs. Norton and her son, Brinsley. But in two letters quoted by Janet Ross in *Three Generations of*

English Women (London, 1888), II, 199, 213, we see Mrs. Norton as she was to her friends, witty, prettily affected and wholly charming. In her later book, *The Fourth Generation* (New York, 1912), Mrs. Ross reproduces the Watts portrait in the Dublin Gallery, gives the family refutation of the *Times* scandal (pp. 351, 352) and on pages 15, 16, 49, 202 shows the famous beauty as she seemed to a clever young girl.

MRS. GORE (CATHERINE MOODY), 1799–1861

Dictionary of Natural Biography (VIII, 236–238); *Illustrated London News,* Feb. 16, 1861, p. 147, contains a portrait

Matthew Whiting Rosa has an excellent chapter on Mrs. Gore in *The Silver-Fork School* (New York, 1936). References to Mrs. Gore may be found in Eliza Lynn Linton's *My Literary Life* (London, 1899) and in Mrs. Oliphant's "Modern Novelists—Great and Small" in *Blackwood's,* May, 1855. Mr. Rosa believes that Mrs. Gore, born Moody, took her stepfather's name of Nevinson. In Henry Chorley's *Letters of Mary Russell Mitford,* I, 36, 37 (London, 1872) Miss Mitford refers to "Miss N's" "very splendid and magnificent wit." Volume I, p. 214, and Vol. II, p. 13 of the same work refer to Mrs. Gore's "thorough worldliness." Charlotte Brontë refused to meet Mrs. Gore! Stephen Wheeler in his *Letters of Walter Savage Landor, Private and Public* (London, 1899) refers to a scandalous story of Mrs. Gore's behavior in Paris, 1841. This cannot be verified, but Janet Ross, whose family knew Mrs. Gore intimately, gives a slight but authentic picture of the novelist and her daughter Cissie (Lady Edward Thynne) in *The Fourth Generation* (New York, 1912), p. 37. Frederick Locker-Lampson in *My Confidences* (New York, 1896), p. 334, speaks of her as "a witty old ghost of the Silver Fork school."

MRS. CRAIK (DINAH MARIA MULOCK), 1826–1887

Dictionary of National Biography (XIII, 1177–1178)

Mrs. Oliphant published an article on Mrs. Craik's life in *Macmillan's Magazine,* December, 1887, probably with the sanction of Mr. Craik, who was a partner in the publishing house. Aleyn Lyell Reade in his sumptuous volume *The Mellards and Their Descendants* (London, 1915), which contains a memoir of Dinah Maria Mulock, discounts much of Mrs. Oliphant's information and presents a picture of a less difficult childhood. His is undoubtedly the most reliable work on the subject. Mrs. Parr wrote on Mrs. Craik in *Women Novelists of Queen Victoria's Reign* (London, 1897). Mrs. Oliphant's *Autobiography* and Mrs. Carlyle's and Miss Mitford's letters have also been of use.

MRS. HENRY WOOD (ELLEN PRICE), 1814–1887

Hammerton's *Concise Universal Biography* (IV, 1416)

Mrs. Wood's son and partner, Charles W. Wood, was the author of the singularly unrevealing *Memorials of Mrs. Henry Wood* (London, 1894). Adeline Sergeant wrote on Mrs. Henry Wood in *Women Novelists of Queen Victoria's Reign* (London, 1897). Arthur Waugh mentions the phenomenon of *East Lynne* in *A Hundred Years of Publishing* (London, 1930).

AMELIA ANN BLANDFORD EDWARDS, 1831–1892

Chambers Biographical Dictionary, p. 331; *Dictionary of National Biography* (XXII, 601–603); A. L. A. Portrait Index, p. 460

Mrs. Macquoid wrote the chapter on "Amelia Edwards" for *Women Novelists of Queen Victoria's Reign* (London, 1897). Miss Edwards' cousin, Matilda Betham Edwards, in her *Reminiscences* (London, 1898), contributed personal recollections. The most interesting information on the subject is contained in an article by C. William Winslow, *The Queen of Egyptology* (pamphlet reprinted from *Antiquarian Magazine*). Harry W. Rudman in *Italian Nationalism and English Letters* (New York, 1940) treats briefly of Miss Edwards' failure to portray the Risorgimento in her *Half a Million of Money*.

MRS. S. C. HALL (ANNA MARIA FIELDING), 1800–1881

Webster's *Biographical Dictionary* (1943) p. 654; Thomas's *Universal Pronouncing Dictionary of Biography and Mythology* (1901; p. 1206)

Her husband's two volumes, *A Book of Memories* (London, 1876) and his *Retrospect of a Long Life* (New York, 1883); Mrs. Howitt's *An Autobiography* (London, 1889); and Mrs. Harry Coghill's *The Autobiography and Letters of Mrs. M. O. W. Oliphant* (London, 1899) furnish information on her life and character. Her good little story *The Old Governess* (London, 1858), "printed and sold for the benefit of the asylum for aged and decayed governesses," is perhaps her best apology. Martin F. Tupper in *My Life as an Author* (London, 1886), pp. 388–394, gives an account of the wonderful séance given by Hume at the Halls' house which converted Samuel and Mrs. Hall from materialism to spiritualism.

MRS. HOWITT (MARY BOTHAM), 1799–1888

Hammerton's *Concise Universal Biography* (III, 785)

Mary Howitt's *An Autobiography* (London, 1889), Bessie Rayner Parkes Belloc's *In a Walled Garden* (London, 1895), S. C. Hall's *Retrospect of a Long Life* (New York, 1883), and the frequently cited *Autobiography* of Mrs. Oliphant contain material on the subject. Mrs. Howitt wrote many children's stories, collaborated with her husband on travel books, and translated numerous titles of Fredrika Bremer and Hans Christian Andersen. Widener Library lists fifty-seven separate works of this prolific author. Mention of the family friendship between the Quaker Howitts and Chorleys is made in Henry G. Hewlett's *Henry Fothergill Chorley: Autobiography, Memoir, and Letters* (London, 1873), I, 217.

THE HONORABLE EMILY LAWLESS, 1845–1913

Dictionary of National Biography (XI, 688); Burke's Peerage, 1939, p. 595; *Who Was Who, 1897–1916*, p. 415; *Webster's Biographical Dictionary* (1943), p. 869

Mrs. Oliphant, who was an intimate friend of Lady Cloncurry, the mother of Miss Lawless, reviewed *Hurrish* in *Blackwood's*, June, 1889, contrasting the simplicity of Miss Lawless with Henry James, who is "all art."

THE HONORABLE EMILY EDEN, 1797–1869

Dictionary of National Biography (VI, 356)

Anthony Eden wrote a biographical, critical introduction to *The Semi-Detached House* (London, 1928). Violet Dickenson's *Miss Eden's Letters* (London, 1919) gives a picture of Miss Eden as a charming, unaffected Englishwoman who passed many years in India.

CHARLOTTE BRONTË, 1816–1855

Two indispensable works on the subject are Elizabeth Gaskell's biography (London, 1857) and Clement K. Shorter's *The Brontës, Life and Letters* (London, 1908), the latter superseding Shorter's *Charlotte Brontë and Her Circle* (New York, 1896). Among modern biographies that by E. F. Benson, *Charlotte Brontë* (London, 1932), makes delightful reading, but his ingenious theory of Branwell's collaboration in *Wuthering Heights* is neatly disproved by Irene Cooper-Willis in *The Authorship of Wuthering Heights* (London, 1936). Miss Cooper-Willis has also written a simple, charming narrative in *The Brontës* (London, 1933). However, Francis A. Leyland first dealt with this subject of disputed authorship in a thoroughly unreliable book, *The Brontë Family* (London, 1886).

The problems raised by the Brontë family have fascinated a number of talented men and women, among whom Ernest Dimnet has written the most authoritative work in *The Brontë Sisters* (English translation, London, 1927). May Sinclair's *The Three Brontës* (London, 1912) attacks Victorian adverse criticism, while Augustine Birrell's brief and elegant *Life of Charlotte Brontë* (London, 1887) is Victorian criticism at its sympathetic best. A. C. Swinburne's *A Note on Charlotte Brontë* (London, 1877) would be more valuable had it not been written to detract from George Eliot's reputation.

Other Victorians whose works have assisted all Brontë scholars are Elizabeth Haldane's *Mrs. Gaskell and Her Friends* (London, 1930), which sheds light on Mr. Brontë and his son-in-law; Margaret Shaen's *Memorials of Two Sisters: Susanna and Catherine Winkworth* (Longman's, 1908);

and Mrs. Ellis H. Chadwick's *In the Footsteps of the Brontës* (London, 1914), which is an excellent study of Brontë places. Sir Thomas Wemyss Reed's *Charlotte Brontë: a Monograph* (London, 1877) is a work of kindly Victorian criticism; while Mrs. Oliphant leads the opposition in "Novelists—Great and Small" (*Blackwood's,* May, 1855), "Literature of the Last Fifty Years" (*Blackwood's,* June, 1887), and ten years later in a chapter of *Women Novelists of Queen Victoria's Reign* (London, 1897).

E. M. Delafield begins her preface to a collection of excerpts, *The Brontës: Their Lives Recorded by Their Contemporaries* (London, 1935), with the observation, "There has been a tendency on the part of all who have ever written about the Brontës to lose their heads," and exemplifies this theory by her own absurdity in calling *Wuthering Heights* a "metaphysical epic." Women more than men are prone to hysteria in treating of the Brontës, probably because of a conviction of being potential Emilys or Charlottes. I have read a good many of these imaginative volumes but would advise no one to follow my example. For those, however, who are interested in the development of the Brontë game such books may be mentioned as John Malham-Dembleby's *The Key to the Brontë Works* (London, 1911), which attributes *Wuthering Heights* to Charlotte; Alice Law's *Patrick Branwell Brontë* (London [1924]), which attributes *Wuthering Heights* to Branwell; Lucile Dooley's *Psychoanalysis of Charlotte Brontë as a Type of the Woman of Genius,* a pamphlet reprinted from the *American Journal of Psychology* (July, 1920), on Charlotte's "father-fixation"; Florence Swinton Day's *Sources of Jane Eyre* (Cambridge, England, 1937), which strips Charlotte of originality; and Virginia Moore's vexatious *The Life and Eager Death of Emily Brontë* (London [1936]), which, without a shred of objective evidence, provides Emily with a Lesbian complex.

The important publications on the *juvenilia* to which I am indebted are Clement Shorter's and C. W. Hatfield's *The Twelve Adventurers* (London [1925]); George E. MacLean's *The Spell* (London, 1931); and Fannie Ratchford's *The Brontës' Web of Childhood* (New York, 1941). The *Transactions and Other Publications of the Brontë Society* (T.B.S.) are also of great value and interest, especially *Charlotte Brontë: 1816–1916,* the Centenary Memorial edited by Butler Wood (London, 1917). Original manuscripts of which I have made use are Charlotte's "Silver Cup, a Tale" and the Brontë children's magazine in Houghton Library, Harvard University, and Charlotte's "Caroline Vernon" and "Henry Hudson and His Sister" in the Harry Elkins Widener Memorial Room, Harvard University.

It seems necessary to add to what is already a tedious list several sources used in the present book which are not so easily available. "The evening comes before the noon" is quoted from C. W. Hatfield's *The Complete Poems of Emily Jane Brontë* (New York, 1941; p. 104). The death of Mrs. Brontë is the subject of the Rev. Patrick Brontë's letter of November, 27, 1821, republished in T.B.S., VII, 284–289 (1931). Aunt Branwell's picture in the possession of Miss Mabel C. Edgerly is reproduced in T.B.S., Vol. IX, No. 2, 1937. Mr. Brontë's letter to the Leeds *Mercury* (November 16, 1844), T.B.S., Vol. VIII, No. 3 (1934), pp. 130–131 claims that he officiated at the funerals of 90 to 100 children who were burned to death while wearing cotton or linen clothes. This extraordinary statement suggests that Brontë inaccuracy was not confined to Charlotte. See also Mr. Brontë's letter to Mrs. Gaskell, July 30, 1857, T.B.S., of Vol. VIII, No. 3 (1934), pp. 129–130.

Eliza and Georgiana in *The Spell* were "tall, haughty blondes, proud of their beauty, proud of their first-rate accomplishments, proud of their lofty lineage, proud of their semi-royal blood, proud of everything." Compare with the Reed sisters in *Jane Eyre*. No. IV of James Hogg's *Tales of Apparitions* is in *Blackwood's*, August, 1827. Dr. MacLean mentions this in his excellent introduction to *The Spell*.

Mabel Edgerly's "Causes of Death of the Brontës," T.B.S., Vol. VIII, No. 3 (1934), is authoritative. In it she reprints a discussion on the cause of Branwell's death from an article in the *British Medical Journal* of April 2, 1932. He is supposed to have begun drinking in 1838. Charlotte's death is attributed to "phthsis—duration two months." Charlotte's correspondence with Hartley Coleridge is dealt with in an article by C. W. Hatfield, T.B.S., 1940. Lady Wilson in "The Brontës as Governesses," T.B.S., Vol. IX, No. 4 (1939), pp. 217–218, suggests the origin of Currer Bell as Currer

Fell, the Yorkshire mountain opposite Eshton Hall, another name used in *Jane Eyre*. On the ideal Victorian lady, see Brontë Society Publications, March 8, 1919, pp. 255-264. Sir W. Robertson Nicoll, "Charlotte Brontë and Anne Mozley," T.B.S., Vol. V, pt. 29, quotes from "Christian Remembrance." Brontë students will find a mine of information in the various publications of the society and the notes from Miss Mabel Edgerly deserve especial praise.

MRS. GASKELL 1810–1865

Gerald De Witt Sanders, *Elizabeth Gaskell*, with a bibliography by Clark S. Northrup (New Haven, 1929) provides a sound foundation for a study of Mrs. Gaskell. Elizabeth Haldane's *Mrs. Gaskell and Her Friends* (London, 1930) and Mrs. Ellis H. Chadwick's *Mrs. Gaskell, Haunts, Homes and Stories* are valuable, though the latter is feebly written. Johanna van Dullemen's *Mrs. Gaskell, Novelist and Biographer* (Holland, 1924) has an admirable first chapter on England in the Industrial Revolution. A. Stanton Whitfield's *Mrs. Gaskell: Her Life and Work* (London, 1929) contains a few letters and some new information but is written in rather puerile style. George A. Payne has published *Mrs. Gaskell; A Brief Biography* (Manchester, 1929) and "Charlotte Brontë's Biographer" in *Transactions of the Brontë Society,* Vol. VII, pt. 40 (1930), pp. 227-237.

Henry James's *William Wetmore Story and His Friends* (New York, 1903), *Letters of Mrs. Gaskell and Charles Eliot Norton, 1855-1865* (London, 1932), and M. L. Parrish's *Victorian Lady Novelists* (London, 1933) all have special value. George Smith's *A Memoir with Some Pages of Autobiography* (London, 1902), p. 29, mentions the exposé of Branwell's love affair; Mary Howitt's "Stray Notes about Mrs. Gaskell" (*Good Words,* XXXVI, 604-612); and Margaret Shaen's *Memorials of Two Sisters: Susanna and Catherine Winkworth* (London, 1908) are indispensable. The letters of Miss Mitford, Mrs. Browning, and Mrs. Carlyle contain many references. Henry G. Hewlett in *Henry Fothergill Chorley* (London, 1873), II, 254, 255, mentions a little known incident characteristic of Mrs. Gaskell's kindness.

GEORGE ELIOT, 1819–1880

J. W. Cross's *George Eliot's Life as Related in Her Letters and Journals* (London, 1885) is indispensable. The excellent though not wholly objective biography by Blanche Colton Williams (New York, 1936) is probably the best modern work on George Eliot's life. Among other more recent publications on the subject are Elizabeth Haldane's temperate *George Eliot and Her Times* (London, 1927); the slight and elegant *Victorian Lady Novelists* (London, 1933) by M. L. Parrish; Anne Fremantle's *George Eliot* (London, 1933); and *Marian* (London, 1939) by Simon Dewes—a pseudonym, and small wonder. I am especially indebted to Anna T. Kitchel's admirable *George Lewes and George Eliot* (New York [1933]) and to Gordon Haight's *George Eliot and John Chapman* (New Haven, 1940).

Contemporary views of the subject are expressed in Margaret Oliphant's "Two Cities—Two Books" (*Blackwood's,* July, 1874); in Mrs. Harry Coghill's *The Life and Letters of Mrs. M. O. W. Oliphant* (London, 1899); Eliza Lynn Linton's *My Literary Life* (London, 1899) and her chapter "George Eliot" in *Women Novelists of Queen Victoria's Reign* (London, 1897); Oscar Browning's *Life of George Eliot* (London, 1890); Matilda Betham Edwards's *Reminiscences* (London, 1898); Mathilde Blind's *George Eliot* (rev. ed., Boston, 1904); Mrs. Humphrey Ward's *A Writer's Recollections* (London, 1918); and Henry James's *Partial Portraits* (London, 1888), which contains a review of Cross's book and the delightful "Daniel Deronda: a Conversation."

George Eliot's *Brother Jacob* and her papers on "The Lady Novelists" and "Woman in France: Madame de Sablé" are republished in her *Works* and in *Essays and Reviews* (Boston, 1887). Frederick Locker-Lampson in *My Confidences* (New York, 1896), pp. 307–318, recalls his personal associations with George Eliot.

MARGARET OLIPHANT, 1828–1897

The incomplete *Autobiography and Letters of Mrs. M. O. W. Oliphant* (London, 1899), edited by her cousin, Mrs. Harry Coghill, is the best source of information. Mrs. Oliphant's own *Agnes* (London, 1866), *A Son of the Soil* (London, 1866), various *Tales of the Unseen,* "The Fancies of a Believer" (*Blackwood's,* February, 1895), an article, "Life on an Island" (*Blackwood's,* Jan., 1865), and a poem, "Day and Night," in the same issue, and a history of the House of Blackwood, *Annals of a Publishing House* (Edinburgh and London, 1897–98), reflect incidents connected with her own life.

J. A. Froude's *Letters and Memorials of Jane Welsh Carlyle* (London, 1883) contains references to Mrs. Oliphant's friendship with Mrs. Carlyle. J. M. Barrie wrote the introduction to her posthumous volume of short stories, *A Widow's Tale* (London, 1898), and gave the address at the unveiling of the memorial in St. Giles's Cathedral which is printed in the collection of Barrie's speeches under the title *M'Connachie and J.M.B.* (London, 1938), pp. 22–26. Denis MacKail in his *The Story of J.M.B.* (London [1941]), pp. 277–403, makes perfunctory mention of Barrie's acquaintance with Mrs. Oliphant. J. M. Dent in his *Memoirs* (London, 1928, pp. 79–80) describes an interview occurring shortly before Mrs. Oliphant's death. C. L. Graves's *Life and Letters of Alexander Macmillan* (London, 1910) expresses the attitude of a great publisher toward her work.

The *Book Buyer,* August, 1893, published a favorable leading article on her; and J. C. Heywood wrote a trashy chapter in his *How They Strike Me, These Authors* (Philadelphia, 1877). A. C. Benson devotes a chapter of his *Memories and Friends* (London, 1924) to his recollection of Mrs. Oliphant and her sons, who were his schoolfellows in Eton. Harriet Waters Preston in *The Library of the World's Best Literature* (Vol. XXVII) gives excerpts from Mrs. Oliphant's works. Hester Ritchie's *Letters of Anne Thackeray Ritchie* (London, 1924) contains references to Mrs. Oliphant's last days. Frederick Locker-Lampson in *My Confidences* (New York, 1896), p. 333, says Trollope told him that if Mrs. Oliphant outlived him (Trollope), she would presently outwrite him. She did outlive him fourteen years.

Index